CHRIS HA...

M000035697

Social Justice Talk

Strategies for Teaching Critical Awareness

Heinemann
Portsmouth, NH

Heinemann
361 Hanover Street
Portsmouth, NH 03801–3912
www.heinemann.com

Offices and agents throughout the world

All ideas and findings in this book represent the perspective of the author and do not necessarily represent the position of Richland School District Two.

"Dedicated to Teachers" is a trademark of Greenwood Publishing Group, Inc.

The author and publisher wish to thank those who have generously given permission to reprint borrowed material:

Figure 1.1: © VISIONS, Inc. Dorchester, MA; for permission to copy/reprint contact 607-541-4100.

Acknowledgments for borrowed material continue on p. 164.

Library of Congress Cataloging-in-Publication Data
Names: Hass, Chris, author.
Title: Social justice talk : strategies for teaching critical awareness / Chris Hass.
Description: Portsmouth, NH : Heinemann, [2020] | Includes bibliographical references.
Identifiers: LCCN 2020018509 | ISBN 9780325112756
Subjects: LCSH: Social justice—Study and teaching (Elementary) | Social Skills—Study and teaching (Elementary)
Classification: LCC LC192.2 .H37 2020 | DDC 370.11/5—dc23

LC record available at https://lccn.loc.gov/2020018509

Editor: Margaret LaRaia
Production: Vicki Kasabian
Interior and cover designs: Vita Lane
Interior photographs: Sherry Day
Author photograph: Tony Claremont
Video production: Dennis Doyle, Paul Tomasyan, Alan Chow
Typesetting: Kim Arney
Manufacturing: Steve Bernier

Printed in the United States of American on acid-free paper
1 2 3 4 5 6 7 8 9 10   VP   25 24 23 22 21 20
August 2020 Printing

This book is dedicated to
every teacher who has ever
chosen what is just
over what is expected.

Contents

Acknowledgments x

Introduction: Love Is Not Enough xiv

Learning to Read the World xv

Essential Understandings for Social Justice Work xvi

🔧 **What We Need to Understand About Self** xvi
🔧 **What We Need to Understand About Society** xvii

My Classroom, My Positionality xvii

Watch ▶ xviii
Clip: The Value in Teacher Restraint
Clip: Conversations for Mutual Respect

1 Identity: Knowing Ourselves 1

🔧 **Where Do You Fall in Historically Excluded and Included Groups?** 2

Social Identity as a Threat to Discussions of Injustice 4

Who Is Given Voice to Speak to These Matters? Who Is Not? 6
Which Perspectives Are Included? Which Are Left Out? 7
Who Gets to Decide What This All Means? Who Does Not? 7

The Trap of the Good/Bad Binary 8

No Teacher Is Immune 11

Navigating Complex Discussions Despite Our Cultural Blinders 12

🔧 **Take Stock of Your Own Social Identities** 13
Engage in Discussions with a Diversity of Peers 14
Access Texts That Expand Your Cultural Competence 15
Engage in Reflective Thought 16

Watch ▶ 17
Clip: Teacher Identity
Clip: The Purpose and Goals of Social Justice Teaching

2 Classrooms That Center Social Critique

19

  🔧 Qualities of Student-Centered Social Justice Conversations   20

Integrated, Not Compartmentalized Social Justice Instruction   21

  Correlating Social Justice Goals with Learning Outcomes   23

  🔧 Correlation of Social Justice Goals with Skills and Strategies   24

Student-Centered Instruction in Action   27

🔧 **Framework for Evaluating Beliefs**   28

  Authority: "I was told by someone I trust."   28

  A Priori: "It just sounds right to me."   29

  Tenacity: "This fits with what I've always believed."   30

  Inquiry: "I need to work hard to make sure this is true."   30

Setting Our Expectations   31

Watch ▶   33

Clip: Connecting History to Contemporary Media

Clip: "Why Haven't They Fixed It Yet?"

3 Identity: Knowing Our Students

35

Inquiring into Our Students' Social Identities   36

🔧 Building and Maintaining Positive Social Identities   37

  Selecting Literature That Reflects the Social Identities of Our Students   38

  Celebrating the Contributions of All   38

  Inviting Family Members into the Class to Share   38

  Using Curriculum to Draw Out Personal Stories   39

A Word About Tools

Understanding that teaching for social justice can be overwhelming, I've offered specific tools throughout this book to help you better focus your work. These tools are marked using the wrench 🔧 symbol.

Inquiring into Our Students' Funds of Knowledge 39

Developing Intentional Practices to Better Know Our Kids 40

Inquiring into the Histories of Our Names 41
Intake Conferences 44
🔧 Intake Conference Questions 44
Family Book Recommendations 45

Watch ▶ 48
Clip: Deep Community Building with Students and Families
Clip: Sharing Our Cultural Knowledge

4 How Children Navigate Diverse Perspectives

51

🔧 Framework for Analyzing Students' Responses to Oppression 52

Students Accepting Injustice 52
🔧 Frames Used for Social Justice Discussions 54
Relationships of Power 55
Socioeconomic power 56
Racial power 57
Analysis 57
Maintenance of the Status Quo 58
Analysis 60
Effect of Learned Stereotypes 62
Analysis 63

Students Denying Injustice 64
The World Is a Fair Place 65
It's Exaggerated or Untrue 68
Analysis 70

Watch ▶ 72
Clip: Expectations for Our Children Over Time
Clip: Challenges in Homogenous Classrooms

5 Using Issue-Based Literature   75

Goal 1: Using Issue-Based Texts to Build Understanding and Empathy   75

Issues That Can Be Explored Through Children's Literature   78

How to Include Empathy and Understanding in Our Reading Curriculum   79

Correlation Between Reading Standards and Social Justice Work   80

Goal 2: Using Issue-Based Texts to Help Students Gain Historical Context   85

Books That Provide Historical Context   87

How to Integrate Historical Context into Our Curriculum   88

Process for Implementing Social Justice into Social Studies Curriculum   88

A Final Word of Caution About Incorporating Issue-Based Texts   91

Watch ▶   93
Clip: Why Issue-Based Literature Works
Clip: "Reading" a Commercial and the Media's Response

6 Placing Social Justice at the Core of Our Morning Meeting   95

Repurposing Our Morning Meeting to Meet the Needs of Social Justice   96

Establishing Classroom Journals   97
(Re)discovering a sense of wonder   100
Modeling how to question the world   101
Generating questions alongside our students   104
Helping students take notice of the questions they're already wondering about   105
Inviting families and caregivers to help generate questions   106

Starting Social Critique with Gender   108

Elevating the Quality of Discussions   110

Positioning Students as Primary Meaning Makers   112

Gradual Release of Responsibility in Classroom Discussions   113

Teaching Moves for Morning Meeting   116

Supporting Students to Listen Closely   119

Scaffolding Students to Build onto the Ideas of Others   123

   Resist the urge to dominate the discussion   124

   Offer stems that promote connections to others' thinking   125

   Selectively call on those who want to make connections   125

Learning to Value the Role of Disagreement in Exploratory Discussions   125

Watch ▶   129

Clip: Using Metaphor and Restatement with Kindergartners

Clip: A Science Journal Entry Leads to Discussion of Ways of Knowing

Clip: Examples of Short Classroom Journal Shares

Clip: Morning Meeting Discussion Strategies

7 Supporting Students to Speak Up
131

Perceived Lack of Knowledge: "I don't have a thought to that question."   133

Provide Our Students the Background Knowledge They Require   135

Prompt Our Students to Share What They're Thinking or Wondering About   136

Fear of Upsetting Others: "I was afraid I might say the wrong thing."   136

Help Our Students See Growth and Understanding as One of Our Primary Goals   138

Model How One Might Respond to Something They Find Offensive   139

   🔧 How to Gently Fold Kids Back In After They've Miscued   141

Discomfort with Hearing Hard Truths: "It's kind of scary."   142

Allow Our Students Space to Decompress and Breathe   144

Carefully Determine What Is Appropriate and What Is Not   144

Lack of Trust in the Teacher: "I don't want to go there with her."   145

Watch ▶   147

Clip: Second Graders Ethan and Kiersten Explain Classroom Journals

Clip: The Slow Process of Learning How to Listen to Each Other

Clip: Valuing Engagement Over Closure

8 When Talk Leads to Action 149

 Framework for Supporting Student Action 150

Actions That Get at the Root Cause(s) of Social Injustice 153

Inquiries That Led to Action: A Collection for Inspiration 154

Watch ▶ 158
Clip: Students Talk on Local News
Clip: Children Find Their Voices and Solutions
Clip: Respect as Activism

Works Cited 159

How to access online videos

To access the online resources for *Social Justice Talk*:

1. Go to **http://hein.pub/sjtalk-login**.

2. Log in with your username and password. If you do not already have an account with Heinemann, you will need to create an account.

3. On the Welcome page, choose "**Click here to register an Online Resource.**"

4. Register your product by entering the code: **JUSTICE** (be sure to read and check the acknowledgment box under the keycode).

5. Once you have registered your product, it will appear alphabetically in your account list of **My Online Resources**.

Note: When returning to Heinemann.com to access your previously registered products, simply log into your Heinemann account and click on "**View my registered Online Resources.**"

Acknowledgments

It's been said we stand on the shoulders of the giants who've come before us. They've led the way, showing us what's possible. For me, these giants take many forms. First and foremost are Heidi Mills and Tim O'Keefe. For more than a decade Heidi Mills has demonstrated an unwavering belief in me as a classroom teacher, a scholar, and an aspiring author. In fact, for a number of years she believed in me far more than I believed in myself. We should all be so lucky as to have a Heidi Mills in our life. Her collaborator and partner in life, Tim O'Keefe, has been equally influential in helping me grow into the teacher my kids and community need me to be. Tim is without doubt one of the very best educators and friends I will ever know. Our daily discussions have taught me more about being a teacher, advocate, and caring human being than any book or degree ever could.

Also among this group of giants are the entire faculty and staff at the Center for Inquiry. I am so fortunate to work alongside such an incredible and passionate group of teachers. It's been their thoughtful insights, rich connections, and critical questions over the years that have pushed me to better understand and articulate my own beliefs about teaching, learning, and the role of education. In particular, I need to recognize Nozsa Tinsley and Tiffany Palmatier. There are few teachers who dedicate themselves so completely to teaching for a more just world. Furthermore, I'm grateful for their willingness to open their classrooms to a Heinemann film crew in support of this book. I know readers will be every bit as grateful to learn from them as I am.

I would also like to show my appreciation for those that have pushed me to develop a more critical awareness of the world around me. At the University of South Carolina, this includes accomplished professors such as Allison Anders, Michele Bryan, and Susi Long, who showed me how to redefine a "safe" classroom as one willing to sacrifice just a bit of personal comfort in exchange for a greater understanding of the world, ourselves, and others. At the New City School, my very first professional home, this includes Tom Hoerr, Barbara Thomson, Julie Stevens, and Joe and Kate Corbett, who helped me not only develop a greater appreciation for the rich diversity found within our communities but also recognize the power each of us has to make a real difference in the lives of others.

I greatly appreciate my editor and friend, Margaret LaRaia. She is truly a giant among giants. Over the past two years she has not only helped me better understand what it means to write with clarity, depth, and function, but has continually shared articles, asked questions, and initiated discussions that forced me to think more reflectively and critically about my teaching. I remember being told early on by a friend who has also worked with Margaret that "she'll make you smarter." This couldn't be truer. Of course, many others have played a key role in making this book a reality. I'm grateful to Janelle Henderson, Carmen Tisdale, Arleigh West, Katy Reardon, and Megan Drayton for investing their time in reading over various drafts and offering insightful feedback. I'm also thankful to all those at Heinemann who lent their expertise to ensure this book would become everything we dreamed it could be. This includes Sherry Day, Dennis Doyle, Vicki Kasabian, Kalli Kilpatrick, Vita Lane, Krysten Lebel, and Paul Tomasyan.

Giants need not always be tall. In fact, sometimes they're only seven or eight years old. As such, I need to extend my fullest gratitude to each and every student who has ever sat alongside me and demonstrated a willingness to engage in critical thought. Most recently, I'd like to acknowledge my current group of students who have dedicated themselves to a multiyear battle to achieve greater equity in our community—a battle that has found them marching up the steps at City Hall and demanding change. Sometimes we win. Other times we need to double our efforts to keep fighting. Either way, we press on together.

Finally, I thank my family. There are no greater giants in my life than them. Considering the significant demands on my time in the evenings and on weekends, this book was most certainly a collaborative effort—not to mention, a collective sacrifice. I'm grateful for the contributions made by my mom, Peggy, who helped out around the house so I could continue working. And my wonderfully understanding children—Harper, Muluken, Ainsley, and Ty—who never made me feel guilty for investing so much time in making this book a reality while also recognizing the efforts I made to work around their schedules. I can't wait to play more games, see more movies, and find new adventures together. And most of all I'm not only thankful but forever indebted to my wife, Tricia, who was far more gracious, patient, and supportive than the self-imposed demands of my endless schedules and deadlines deserved. I wish so much I could dig deep inside and discover some inner E. B. White hiding within me that could script the eloquent words you deserve. But you know me better than that. So I'll say simply that I love you with all my heart and am so thankful for all you do. There are no stronger shoulders than yours.

Who We Are

As will be explored in great detail over the course of this book, who we are matters. Our identities, lived experiences, and developing perspectives not only shape how we experience the world but how we go about defining the work we do in our classrooms. For this reason, we want to share with you, the reader, a little bit about ourselves. I, Chris, am the primary author of this book. Both Tiffany and Nozsa are colleagues of mine whose work continually inspires and transforms my own understandings of teaching for social justice. Their reflections on teaching for social justice can be seen, alongside my own, in the videos that accompany this text.

I (Chris Hass) grew up in a small steel town located in southwestern Illinois. At that time my community consisted largely of white, working-class families. Racism, homophobia, sexism, xenophobia, and a whole host of other oppressive worldviews were the norm in most homes. This in no way made our community unique. Rather, this oppressive worldview plagued (and continues to plague) many towns and cities across the country.

Like many other white children growing up at that time, my passivity played an important role in maintaining this ideology of hate. A product of my environment, I learned firsthand what it means to blindly accept the beliefs that surround you without stopping to question whether any of this is true, who it benefits, or the harm it does to others. Looking back, I feel regret. I regret I wasn't strong enough to tell people, "That joke isn't funny," as they laughed at the expense of others. I regret I didn't say, "That's hateful," as they belittled people different from themselves. And I regret I was largely willing to look the other way so many times.

But while I have regrets, I do not feel shame. Over time I grew to know better, so I did better. In the thirty years since, I've worked to surround myself with people from all walks of life who are willing to challenge me to identify and reflect upon the implicit biases society has embedded within my psyche. In turn, I hope I do the same for others. We are on this journey together and we'll likely never reach the end. My hope as a classroom teacher is that I can help my students choose a similar path for themselves.

• • • • •

I (Tiffany Palmatier) was born and raised in a small rural town in South Carolina. My town's biggest attraction was the local flea market, where I watched my grandmother interact with one of the few white people I'd seen my family communicate with on a regular basis. Through my family's rich storytelling tradition, I'd overheard countless stories that positioned the "white man" as untrustworthy and racist.

During my elementary years, many of my teachers were white. Unfortunately, my early experiences with these white teachers ran parallel to the narratives I'd already heard so many times. At a very young age, I remember feeling that I was less than because my family, although rich in love and support, lacked financial resources. Thankfully, this pattern was interrupted during my seventh-grade year, when we relocated to Columbia, South Carolina, so my mom could start a new job and provide my sister and me with more opportunities. Although I love my hometown, this move changed my life in the most beautiful way. For the first time, I experienced powerful, encouraging teachers (both white and Black) who challenged my thinking and believed in me. These rich experiences continued throughout high school and college. Looking back now, I realize my world back home was so small. I didn't have the positive experiences with white people I needed to offset the negative ones.

I know the impact a teacher can have on a student's life—unfortunately, the negative and the positive. My goal as an early childhood teacher is to celebrate each child's identity, help them build an awareness of the greater world, and encourage them to act when they feel compelled to do so. There is no better place to start this crucial work than kindergarten and first grade.

· · · · ·

I (Nozsa Tinsley) grew up in a small town in South Carolina with many mom-and-pop stores; some where young Black girls like myself felt welcomed and others where they didn't. Our small town was like many others throughout the country with a variety of parades and festivals throughout the year to bring the community together. Yet, even in these beautiful moments where many cultures came together in the same space, there was still a clear divide. Races weren't mixing so much as they were existing in parallel. The same was true in our neighborhoods, schools, and churches.

I grew up in a very pro-Black household where I was encouraged to embrace my skin, my language, and my culture. I was taught I needed to work twice as hard as my white peers and was encouraged to tone down my Blackness outside the safety and comfort of my home and community. I also grew up hearing terrible stories about my family's experiences with white people. These stories often included a number of generalizations. Before long I'd internalized many stereotypes about white people. These same stereotypes were only strengthened through my own negative experiences at school.

These perceptions weren't really challenged until much later, during my time as a graduate student and a classroom teacher. The stereotypes I'd learned and internalized were slowly broken down through many amazing interactions with those around me. This is what I want to provide my students, a place where their own generalizations and stereotypes can be challenged through conversations and classroom studies.

Introduction
Love Is Not Enough

What does it mean to teach for social justice? If you had asked me this question many years ago, I likely would've told you it means to teach our children to love all others—not despite their differences but *including* them. At the time, I wholeheartedly believed a multicultural curriculum was the solution to confronting racism, xenophobia, sexism, homophobia, and the myriad of other oppressive ideologies at play within our society. Teaching students to respect and appreciate all people, I thought, was *the* solution to combating the injustices, both subtle and blatant, so many experience on a daily basis. I was wrong.

My error was in oversimplifying the systems of oppression interwoven into the fabric of our society. Good, loving people unknowingly contribute to systems of oppression every day. *I* unknowingly contribute to systems of oppression every day. So do you. Given this, it's not enough to care for or even love someone. Love alone doesn't protect marginalized communities from the effects of systemic injustice nor does it guarantee we ourselves are somehow free from maintaining these very systems, directly or indirectly, through our own unexamined beliefs and actions.

I was reminded of the limitations of love a few years ago when talking to a friend about a local incident at a neighboring high school. A white school resource officer had been caught on video using extreme force on a Black female student. I believed the officer's violent actions came from seeing students of Color as inherently more threatening, and thus deserving of greater force, than most white students. This was supported by documented accusations made against him previously from other people of Color in the community. This history of violence made little difference to my friend as she drew upon the notion of goodness—the ability to love—to claim racism had nothing to do the school resource officer's motives. "I just don't buy it," she argued. "He can't be racist. His *girlfriend* is Black." Her understanding of racism was informed by the belief that loving an individual person means one can no longer hold any preconceived notions about the groups to which they belong. I was quick to point out that in our lifetimes both she and I had known quite a few men who were incredibly sexist yet married to women they cared for deeply. No, love is not enough. Not to overcome centuries of learned prejudice and discriminatory action.

But if not love, what else? Let me begin by saying love *is* an essential piece of the social justice puzzle. It's vital that students learn to better understand and value all people of the world. This begins with recognizing and celebrating what each child brings with them to the classroom. If a social justice education is one dedicated to building a more just society, then we have to begin by helping our children build positive social identities using their cultural knowledge and histories, while also extending these same efforts to better understanding and appreciating the diversity all around us.

So yes, teaching love—love for oneself and love for others—is a great place to begin. But if we truly want to disrupt societal injustices, we have to boldly push into cultural criticism. We have to help students first question then disassemble the particular beliefs and practices that maintain oppression. In doing so, we begin to expand what it means to teach for social justice.

Learning to Read the World

This book will detail how to facilitate rich discussions that disrupt the harmful social beliefs and practices that maintain injustice. To accomplish this, you'll learn how to work alongside your students to *read the world*. As advocated by critical theorist Paulo Freire (1970), reading the world calls on us to become mindful observers who question and critique all we see. This integral work allows students to begin noticing and naming the practices they feel are unfair (say, the overrepresentation of white males in the Oval Office) and then identifying what beliefs create these unjust conditions and even make them seem inevitable or natural in the eyes of many. This act of noticing and naming is essential. Our primary goal is generative critique that allows students to continue noticing, questioning, and critiquing far beyond the reaches of our classrooms.

It's important to recognize this practice of reading the world, rooted in a critical curiosity that promotes student-led questioning and meaning making, goes against the grain of what we've learned classrooms and teacher–student relationships should be. It's not often teachers allow their students' questions to guide the curriculum or their tentative understandings to count as legitimate knowledge. Classrooms are often places where students blindly accept the wishes, knowledge, and perspectives of the teacher. But what does this get us? Too often, it produces silent spaces where students not only become detached and cynical but also learn to become passive receivers of information. This robs students of valuable opportunities to develop critical thinking skills and the sense of agency they'll need to take proactive stances in the future. Cornelius Minor (2019) astutely points out that we'll achieve a more just society not through our content but through our methodology. If our methodology is one that positions learners to remain silent and to willfully accept all they are provided—in the classroom and out—we will never achieve our goals of creating a better and more just democracy.

Essential Understandings for Social Justice Work

As with any author, I'm going to make certain assumptions about my readers. I assume you're genuinely interested in helping students learn to identify, explore, and address issues of injustice in the classroom and beyond. And I assume you're willing to push yourself to grow just as much as your students, if not more so. Yet, before we can begin this work, I first need to establish some essential understandings that underscore all efforts to address issues of social justice in the classroom. Read over them closely while carefully considering their meaning to you on a personal level as well as to your classroom teaching.

 Tool

What We Need to Understand About Self

- Growing up in this society has caused me to unknowingly develop prejudices. Having these prejudices does not make me a bad person. However, I do have a responsibility to acknowledge and dismantle each of these as they reveal themselves to me over time.

- There are times when I'm so used to things being the way they are I fail to recognize the presence of injustice or oppression in the lives of others. Yet, just because I've not been aware of these myself does not mean they aren't real.

- There's no such thing as being neutral. Any attempts on my part to avoid facing hard truths or engaging in critical work alongside my students only serves to support the many systems of oppression at play within our society. My silence and inaction make me complicit in the harm done to others.

- I shouldn't mistake my comfort for my safety. The same is true for my students. This is hard work and I should expect it to push each of us in ways we're not used to being pushed. Though it is uncomfortable at times, it's necessary for real growth and change.

- I'm unlikely to see an end to racism, sexism, xenophobia, and most other forms of oppression in my own lifetime. Yet, all the same, I'm willing to do the work because small victories, accumulated over time, bring us closer to a more just society.

What We Need to Understand About Society

- Oppressive beliefs and practices are intended to maintain unjust power imbalances in our society so those within the dominant culture can protect their privilege. Furthermore, deliberate efforts are made to protect these privileges.

- Our actions as individuals are heavily influenced by the larger social systems to which we belong. These social systems (neighborhood, school, religious/spiritual community, and so on) shape our understanding of the world and how to live in it. Were we to live within other social systems, we would likely view and experience the world differently. For this reason, the way we make sense of the world is no more than a singular view of *reality* and one that could be expanded by spending more time listening to and learning from others who are different from us.

- Race, ethnicity, sexuality, gender, and all other means of grouping people are not based on any proven science but, rather, socially constructed. There are countless other ways people could be grouped instead and those currently in use within our society hold no more credibility than these other possibilities (say, handedness, hair color, height, or agility).

My Classroom, My Positionality

The classroom transcriptions and vignettes in this book come directly from discussions and engagements I've had alongside second- and third-grade students over the past ten years. To make sense of these structures and those participating within them, it's important to take a moment to provide some information about myself, my classroom, and my kids. Who we are matters. It matters because our perspectives, investments, desires, and fears provide the lens through which we see the world—and critique it.

Several years ago, I gave a presentation about this work to a group of educators. After spending an hour sharing student artifacts, classroom vignettes, and feedback from families, a professor of Color from the nearby state university raised her hand and asked, "Because we don't see a whole lot of white teachers talking about race in the classroom, could you speak to how being white affects your ability to discuss race with a diverse group of kids?" With just a couple moments left before attendees were to move on to other sessions, I felt the gravity of this question weighing on me

Watch ▶

The Value in Teacher Restraint: In this clip, Chris reflects on the importance of teacher restraint in social justice teaching.

Conversations for Mutual Respect: Parent Judi talks about how the conversations that happen among children in school are transformational for society.

and I fumbled it. Badly. Speaking to what my whiteness meant in regard to how families had accepted, questioned, or challenged our classroom's social justice work in the past, I failed to address the most critical aspect of her concern: *How can someone of privilege, having never personally experienced the effects of individual or systemic racism, speak from a position of authority within a group of children for whom these discussions are not just academic but extremely personal?*

This is a question I grapple with on a daily basis when engaged in critical discussions with my students. It's imperative that I'm always aware that I speak from a position of privilege as a result of my whiteness within discussions of race, my maleness within discussions of gender, and my heterosexuality within discussions of relationships and family structures. As will be discussed at multiple points throughout this book, the perspectives I take and the importance I give to particular aspects of a current event or student question are largely based on the limitations of my own experiences. That's not to say I don't know a good bit about these topics. I do. However, in each case my understanding is detached because my knowledge has come from discussions with friends, family members, colleagues, and peers as well as a large collection of observations, films, speeches, books, articles, and so on. I have no lived experiences to help me truly understand what it means to be Black, female, gay, trans, Muslim, wheelchair bound, or a refugee, to name just a few.

No matter who you are, this will always be the case. Each of our students represents an intersection of the many social groups to which they belong. For this reason, we cannot—and should not—ever allow ourselves to assume we are an authority capable of resolving our students' every question or concern. In fact, one of my primary goals in writing this book is to help you see the power and importance of placing your kids at the forefront of the meaning-making process. Our kids provide a diversity of experiences and thought that are invaluable to the collaborative nature of this work.

The students represented in this text, a composite spread out across multiple classes over the years, constitute a diverse group. My classrooms are typically 50 percent white, 45 percent Black, and 5 percent Asian-American. The vast majority of children are active Christians and a small handful are Jewish, Muslim, or atheist. With regard to the political leanings of families, I teach in the Southeast, which is an ideologically conservative region. That said, based on pieces of information that find their way into our classroom discussions about a variety of topics, including upcoming elections, the families in my classroom seem to be about two-thirds liberal and one-third conservative. About 25 percent of students in my classroom receive free or reduced lunch. I don't share any of these statistics in an effort to have you paint a picture in your mind of who you think my students are in relation to your own. None of these statistics fully tell the story of my children, their families, or our community. However, this information does provide some context to better situate the work presented on these pages.

Identity
Knowing Ourselves

1

For many years researchers willed themselves to believe their identities didn't matter. They didn't acknowledge that who they were influenced how they viewed the world and that this played an unspoken role in their research—from how participants interacted with them to how they interpreted their data. Thankfully, much has changed over the past few decades—at least in the social sciences. One example of this is the research Jonathan Harvey (2013) has conducted into the experiences of people rehabilitating from severe traumatic brain injuries. As someone who's sustained a traumatic brain injury himself, Harvey understands his identity as a survivor helps him more easily catch nuances when listening to the experiences of other traumatic brain injury survivors. Yet, at the same time, his insider status poses the threat he might misinterpret other survivors' experiences through the lenses of his own journey to rehabilitation. The identities and experiences of researchers cannot help but have an impact on how they make sense of everything they see, hear, and do in the field.

The same, of course, is true of teachers. Teaching for social justice requires you to acknowledge that who you are plays a significant role in your work—from how you interpret your kids' questions to how you make sense of issues facing your communities. To gain a better sense of how the particulars of your social identity shape the work you do in the classroom, select an aspect of your identity from Figure 1.1 that places you within the dominant culture of American society (listed here as "Non-Target"). I'm defining dominant culture here as the cultural practices or ways of being that hold the most power or privilege in American society.

Where Do You Fall in Historically Excluded and Included Groups?

Types of Oppression	Variable	Non-Target Groups	Target Groups
Racism	Race/Color/Ethnicity	White	People of Color (African, Asian, Indigenous, Latinx)
Classism	Socioeconomic status	Middle, Upper Class	Poor, working class
Elitism	Education Level/ Place in Hierarchy	Formally educated, Managers, Exempt, Faculty	Informally educated, Clerical, Nonexempt, Students
Sexism	Gender	Men	Women, Transgender, Intersex
Cissexism/ Transphobia	Gender Identity/ Gender Expression	Cisgender, Appearance and behaviors are congruent with the Gender Binary System	Transgender, gender nonconforming, genderqueer, nonbinary gender
Heterosexism	Sexual Orientation	Heterosexuals	Gay, Lesbian, Bisexual, Pansexual, Asexual, Queer, Questioning
Religious Oppression	Religion	Christians/ Protestants	Muslim, Jewish, Catholic, Agnostic, Hindu, Atheist, Buddhist, Spiritual, LDS, Jehovah's Witness, Pagan
Anti-Semitism	Religion and Culture	Non-Jewish	Jewish
Militarism	Military Status	WWI and II, Gulf War veterans	Vietnam, Iraq, Afghanistan veterans, Pacifists
Ageism/Adultism	Age	Young Adults, Adults	Elders (40+ by law), Children
Ableism	Physical, Mental, Emotional, Learning Ability	Currently able-bodied	People with a physical, mental, emotional, and/or learning disability

Where Do You Fall in Historically Excluded and Included Groups?

Types of Oppression	Variable	Non-Target Groups	Target Groups
Xenophobia	Immigrant Status	U.S. born	Immigrant
Linguistic Oppression	Language	English	English as a second language, Non-English

© VISIONS, Inc. Dorchester, MA; for permission to copy/reprint contact 617-541-4100.

Note: *Please note that this chart is not presented as definitive, authoritative, or "the right or only way," but rather as a meaningful starting and reference point for a common language and approach to dialogue.*

Figure 1.1
Where Do You Fall in Historically Excluded and Included Groups?

I'll engage in this practice alongside you, selecting my gender (male). Now mentally list all the unearned privileges you're afforded solely for being part of this particular social group. I'll warn you, unless you're used to this kind of analysis, it can be challenging at first. This is because over the course of your lifetime you've likely never been forced to reflect on such realities. Not having to think about the ways society works in your favor is, in itself, a privilege. Here's a small sampling of my privileges as a male member of American society:

- I can expect others to focus on my intellect and character rather than my body, age, or style.

- I can expect others to accept my strength and physical capabilities without surprise and without the use of the qualifier "for a boy."

- I can expect to struggle with something new without having this be seen as a deficit of my entire gender.

- I can expect to be granted implicit and explicit messages of my importance and power on a regular basis (i.e., overrepresentation in street names, memorials, and statues as well as overrepresentation in legislative, managerial, and boardroom roles, and so on).

- I can expect the historical contributions of my gender to be placed at the center of all mandated curricula.

- I can expect legislative issues to be taken up from a male perspective.

- I can expect to enter nearly every field of study or profession without fear for how I might fit in or be treated by colleagues based on my gender.

- I can expect greater chances of reaching positions of power and influence within most every profession than my female counterparts.

- I can expect that no one will be surprised by my success in a given field.

- I can expect that my assertiveness in the workplace will not be met with efforts to label me as aggressive, overbearing, or a "bitch."

When I was first pressed to consider the privileges I'm gifted as a male, I was already aware of many. Certainly, I knew men are better represented in politics and dominate positions of power in most professional fields. But there were a number of others I'd never considered (say, the fact my struggles won't be seen as a condemnation of the abilities of *all* males). Suddenly aware of these "hidden" truths, I rushed to share them with my wife, thinking for certain she'd be blown away by the sheer number of male privileges we fail to recognize even exist. Turns out the *we* was just *me*. As a woman, she'd known this all along. She patiently heard me out and casually responded, "Uh, yeah!" At that moment I realized I'd been living in a protective bubble of ignorance. This bubble protected me from having to confront my own privilege or consider my own role in the daily maintenance of these injustices. This meant that I could love a person (or even an entire group of people) and still unwittingly hold beliefs and take daily actions that work to oppress them. As teachers who facilitate daily discussions around injustice, we *must* become increasingly aware of the aspects of daily life we've failed to recognize as a result of our own social identities. To successfully teach for social justice, it's critical we first acknowledge the blinders we wear and then work to remove them. The purpose of this chapter is to help you begin this work.

Social Identity as a Threat to Discussions of Injustice

Earlier, I shared the story of a presentation where someone asked, "Because we don't see a whole lot of white teachers talking about race in the classroom, could you speak to how being white affects your ability to discuss race with a diverse group of kids?" If you'll remember, I fumbled this question badly. The truth is I wasn't wholly prepared for it. Though the significance of my whiteness (and maleness, heterosexuality, and so on) were topics I reflected on quite often, I hadn't realized just *how* important all these were in relation to my role as a facilitator of discussions around injustice. I'm not alone in this. Many white teachers walk blindly into discussions of race without first understanding the dangers their social identities pose to potential outcomes. No matter how much we work to create classrooms where everyone has a voice that's valued, we can never escape the fact we, as the teacher, have an incredible amount of power when it comes to creating new knowledge in the classroom. For example, consider the following hypothetical scenario playing out in an elementary classroom. While doing so, see if you can identify the moves Mrs. Miller, a middle-class white woman, makes that are well intentioned yet work to affirm an oppressive narrative about law enforcement and communities of Color (Figure 1.2).

Mrs. Miller describes herself as an ally to all marginalized groups. She uses culturally relevant teaching that includes helping her students begin to question and take action against injustice. As part of this work, she embeds daily opportunities for her kids to share current news articles. One morning a handful of her students, after hearing multiple stories over the course of the year about interactions between police officers and unarmed Black men, began questioning why so many unarmed Black men were being falsely arrested, brutalized, and even killed by local police. Unsure how to respond, Mrs. Miller did her best to assure them they were safe and that such incidents would be investigated.

Near the end of the school year Mrs. Miller accepted an offer from one of the children's parents to visit the classroom and read a book. This guest, by chance, was a white police officer who showed up in full uniform. After the read-aloud was finished, the kids were given an opportunity to ask questions. One young Black boy raised his hand and bravely asked, "How come the police keep killing all these Black people who don't even have a gun?" The room fell silent. As Mrs. Miller shifted uneasily in her chair, the children's faces turned slowly back to the officer to see what he had to say. The officer took a moment to consider his response and then explained how difficult and complex these situations can be and assured the kids police officers react based on their training, not an intention to harm any particular group of people. He pointed to the beautiful diversity of faces found in the classroom and explained his job is to help maintain safe communities for all people no matter their race. Mrs. Miller politely thanked the officer for coming and breathed a sigh of relief after getting him out the door.

The next day the young boy returned to school with a news article to share. His article detailed how days of silent protest in Baltimore had turned to rioting in some parts of the city in the wake of a funeral for Freddie Gray—a Black man who'd recently died of a spinal cord injury while in police custody. A diversity of ideas emerged as the kids sat around the circle sharing what they'd heard about the case, the protests, and the riots. They asked questions of one another and debated whether or not it was right for people to be destroying businesses and burning cars. It was a rich opportunity to make sense of what was happening in the company of a diversity of peers. To wrap up the discussion, Mrs. Miller reminded her students of the officer's visit the day before and the fact the police serve and protect our communities in many ways. She ended by saying, "And I think we can all agree that violence is never the answer. People can be upset but they need to protest peacefully—just as Dr. Martin Luther King Jr. taught us."

Figure 1.2

Mrs. Miller: How One Perspective Limits Truth

We can all applaud teachers like Mrs. Miller for having the courage to explore critical issues alongside their kids. In a time when the realities of high-stakes standardized testing tend to narrow the curriculum, these teachers buck this trend to ensure their students develop as civic beings invested in the problems facing their local, national, and global communities. However, as well intentioned as Mrs. Miller may have been in facilitating an exploration into the topic of police violence, the limitations of her cultural lenses as a white woman and the power she held in determining how meaning was constructed in her classroom created a very troubling result. Her intentions to create meaning with her kids were derailed when, despite her own limited understanding of this topic, she took a key role in creating meaning *for* her students in three critical (and dangerous) ways. Specifically, she:

1. determined who was (and was not) given voice by virtue of classroom visits
2. controlled what perspectives would be allowed as potential truths during class discussions
3. used her power to claim the final word in naming what should ultimately be taken away from these discussions.

This power to create meaning for students should *always* be brought into question because our social identities—as determined by our race, ethnicity, religion, and a whole host of other social groups to which we belong—inform how we view a particular event or issue. To fully understand this, let's consider how Mrs. Miller's social identity as a white teacher informed the decisions she made.

Who Is Given Voice to Speak to These Matters? Who Is Not?

First, the only two voices of authority granted an opportunity to explain their perspectives on police brutality both came from white members of the community. One was the police officer and the other was Mrs. Miller herself. One way we create new beliefs is through authority—having a trusted source tell us something is true. We can assume it was not Mrs. Miller's intention to silence Black voices as sources of authority on matters of race relations, policing, and forms of protest. Yet this is precisely what she did.

Which Perspectives Are Included? Which Are Left Out?

Second, Mrs. Miller failed to consider the officer's explanation from a perspective other than her own. In doing so, she did not allow her students to explore the tensions that often exist between communities of Color and law enforcement. Had Mrs. Miller been a teacher of Color or had a greater understanding of cultural bias, she would have been more likely to ask the officer follow-up questions about learned prejudices and the role they play, consciously or not, in the way we read particular situations and people. In failing to do so, the officer's perspective that the law enforcement community doesn't act based on their own biases (something *all* of us do every day whether we are aware of it or not) went unchecked and unchallenged—both in the moment during his visit and within the class discussion the following day.

Who Gets to Decide What This All Means? Who Does Not?

Lastly, despite the fact that Baltimore has a long, troubled history of police brutality, unequal justice, and economic disparities leading to significantly shorter life spans for those living in Black neighborhoods, Mrs. Miller's summative takeaway from the class discussion ("violence is never the answer") failed to acknowledge that these important contextual realities existed and ultimately placed the blame back on the Black community for having some among them so angry and fed up with it all they felt the only power they had left was to put their anger on full display. In a discussion that built upon centuries of oppression and brutality perpetrated on Brown bodies, Mrs. Miller not only avoided addressing acts of police brutality raised by a young Black student but also tasked those within the Black community with peacefully accepting such abuse. Yes, violence as a response to injustice should always be questioned and critiqued. But when this questioning and critique occur in the absence of a parallel inquiry into the centuries of violence leading to such riots, we have whitewashed any efforts to help students truly understand the complexity of the issues so many face today. Therein lies the problem with Mrs. Miller—or any other teacher drawing on their own limited experiences and knowledge—when attempting to boil complex social issues down to a single learning outcome.

The Trap of the Good/Bad Binary

How does this happen? As demonstrated in the previous vignette, a great deal of it has to do with our inability to see outside of ourselves. We fail to acknowledge our understanding of a given issue as just that—*our* understanding. It's not until we begin to question our personal beliefs (from how they were developed to whether or not they are even true) that we begin to create opportunities for true growth and learning. Yet, in discussions of race this is often difficult for white teachers. Becoming reflective of our own beliefs inevitably leads to the realization that not only are some of our beliefs not true but some are rooted in underlying prejudices. Prejudices—the preconceived notions each of us hold that aren't based on any real knowledge or experience—frighten us because we have a tendency to see these within the context of a good/bad binary.

The good/bad binary, as explained in Robin DiAngelo's book *White Fragility: Why It's So Hard for White People to Talk About Racism* (2018), is constructed upon the belief that to hold prejudices automatically makes one a bad person. Therefore, to be viewed as "good" one must do all one can to demonstrate purity of thought when it comes to race, gender, sexuality, ethnicity, and so on. The problem with this is twofold. For one, it assumes we can somehow navigate the social systems we inhabit while remaining unaffected by the endless supply of negative messages we receive about difference on a daily basis. One step we can take to avoid derailing discussions of injustice and inequity is to admit to the fact we hold certain prejudices—even if we're not aware of them. These prejudices have been shaped by the cultural lenses through which we see the world. Speaking to how these cultural lenses develop, DiAngelo explains

> I can be told everyone is equal by my parents, I can have friends of color, and I may not tell racist jokes. Yet, I am still affected by the forces of racism as a member of a society in which racism is the bedrock. I will still be seen as white, treated as white, and experience life as a white person. My identity, personality, interests, and investments will develop from a white perspective. I will have a white worldview and a white frame of reference. In a society in which race clearly matters, our race profoundly shapes us. (2018, 72–73)

The second problem with the good/bad binary is that any efforts to see ourselves or have others see us as "good" only serve to keep us from thinking critically about our own role in maintaining systems of oppression. Likely, this was a barrier for Mrs. Miller. Her desire to protect the "goodness" of the white police officer (and by extension, herself as a fellow white person) kept her from helping her students demand a more honest discussion about the role of implicit biases and their relationship to patterns of harassment, racial profiling, and police brutality across the nation. Furthermore, she could have turned this on herself and spoken to the ways her own actions and inactions allow these prejudices to continue—beginning with the fact she had attempted to remain neutral when it came to discussions of police brutality and had avoided offering public support of organizations such as Black Lives Matter in a show of solidarity with communities of Color and their fight for improved policing and justice. Of course, to make this concession Mrs. Miller would first have to come to the realization all whites, by virtue of their racial blinders, play a role in the brutalization of Black and Brown bodies whether or not they're the ones brandishing a weapon or throwing a punch. Figure 1.3 details the decisions Mrs. Miller unknowingly made to affirm an oppressive narrative that places blame on the Black community while turning a blind eye to the injustices thrust upon them not only by law enforcement but by our society as a whole.

Event	Mrs. Miller's Choice of Action	The Result	Other Possibilities That Were Available
A young Black child asks the classroom guest (a white police officer) why unarmed Black men are being shot by police.	• Sits and listens, without comment, as the police officer explains that law enforcement reacts based solely on their training and without any intention to harm particular groups of people	• Silences Black voices and experiences while the singular perspective of a white police officer is allowed to define the reality of the policing of Brown and Black bodies • Constructs meaning for students (through authority) without further critique or questioning	• Ask follow-up questions of the officer about the presence of learned prejudices that affect how we respond to various people and situations • Invite a diversity of speakers to share their own experiences and understandings of the tensions between law enforcement and communities of Color • Invite kids to continue these discussions at home and report back to the class
The same student shares an article about riots developing in Baltimore in response to the death of Freddie Gray.	• Provides an opportunity for kids to share what they've heard about the case as well as ask follow-up questions of one another	• Positions students as primary meaning makers who expect to collaboratively explore issues in their communities, the nation, and the world • Teaches children to be curious and to care about what is going on around them • Allows students to engage with multiple perspectives and speak back to those things that do not make sense or trouble them	

(continues)

Event	Mrs. Miller's Choice of Action	The Result	Other Possibilities That Were Available
The same student shares an article about riots developing in Baltimore in response to the death of Freddie Gray.	• Reminds students of the officer's visit and message from the day before	• Uses the officer's authority to support her own accepted narrative about the relationship between race and policing (thus, a white person referencing another white person to explain the experiences of the black community) • Reaffirms the officer's authority and ability to create meaning for the class without any further questioning or critique • Protects the status of whites as "good"	• Explain to students the limitations of hearing only one perspective on an issue—especially when that perspective comes from the dominant group rather than those being marginalized and oppressed • Ask students who else they need to hear from to better understand the complexity of this issue • Invite people of Color to come in and speak to their experiences and understandings around this issue
	• Wraps up the discussion by taking the final word and explaining violence is never the answer	• Positions teacher as the primary meaning maker even when discussing a topic with which she has little to no personal experience • Whitewashes the complexity of the issue by boiling everything down to a single, oversimplified talking point • Places blame firmly on the Black community for protesting in a fashion unacceptable to Mrs. Miller (despite the fact similar responses from the white community are celebrated when studying protests and acts of defiance during events such as the American Revolution) • Ignores all that has happened both historically and in the present to bring about such anger and hostility from certain protestors	• Avoid the desire to always have the final word—especially about topics where she has no firsthand knowledge • Invite students to learn more about this topic together and to collaboratively develop the big ideas they feel are most important • Identify her role in maintaining a society that allows communities of people to be judged based on implicit biases • Instead of wrapping up the discussion with a final word and providing false closure, ask students what they should work to do as individuals and as a class to address some aspect of this problem

Figure 1.3

Analysis of Mrs. Miller's Approach

No Teacher Is Immune

Our social identities and cultural lenses affect all of us no matter our race, ethnicity, gender, sexuality, religion, or socioeconomic status. There are two reasons for this:

1. Many forms of injustice are at play in our society and we are positioned differently to each of these.

2. Our social identities are not singular because they exist at the intersection of the multiple social groups to which we belong.

While a Black, Christian teacher might find times when their own identities align them with a marginalized group in relation to one issue (systemic racism), there will be times when this same teacher is positioned as part of the dominant social group in relation to other issues (say, religious persecution). Just because someone knows what it's like to be oppressed based on the color of their skin does not mean they have an equal understanding of what it means to live as a Muslim in post–9/11 America. Yes, Black Americans can certainly empathize with many of the emotions, frustrations, and fears the Muslim community experiences, but unless they are Muslim themselves, they will inevitably have their own cultural blind spots and prejudices to overcome when addressing the specifics of such issues. Third-grade teacher Nozsa Tinsley knows this feeling of separation between our own experiences and those of students who experience the world differently than she does as a Black woman. In speaking to a particularly challenging class discussion immediately following the 2016 presidential election, she explains:

> I taught at a school consisting mostly of Black and Brown students. As the students trickled in, you could feel the sadness that came from seeing Donald Trump elected. I decided to let the emotions happen because it needed to be processed. As we gathered on the carpet for Morning Meeting, I could just tell this was going to be a long discussion.
>
> Each of the kids shared how sad and angry they were. To be honest, I shared those same emotions. Yet, I was surprised when one of my kids told us he was not sad or angry. He was afraid. At first, I was confused. I asked him to tell us more. He explained how certain he was his family was going to be sent back to Mexico. I wanted to tell him it probably wouldn't happen. I wanted to tell him politicians say lots of things to get elected they don't follow through with. But most importantly I wanted to convince him he shouldn't worry or be afraid. But I couldn't. His wasn't an emotion I could directly relate to. I didn't know what it meant to live with a fear of deportation.
>
> What was most important during this Morning Meeting was listening, empathizing, and creating a safe space for his thoughts and emotions to

be voiced. As teachers, we don't have all the answers or even relatable experiences to draw upon. But as compassionate humans we have the capability to set aside what we think we know to allow students to let us know how they feel.

Even if we share membership within a particular social group, it doesn't mean our individual experiences and understandings are universal to all others within the same group. This is due, in part, to the intersectionality of our identities. Intersectionality speaks to the fact we are more than just our race. We are more than just our gender. Our identities lie at the confluence of the many groups to which we belong (our religion, class, sexual preference, education, and so on)—though some will have much greater social ramifications on our daily experiences than others. On top of this, the experiences each of us within a particular social group brings to a given topic (such as racism) will differ. As a kindergarten and first-grade teacher, Tiffany Palmatier wrestles with this on a regular basis. She toes the line between helping her students understand how race is taken up in America and acknowledging she could never offer a definitive voice on this or any other related topic. She explains:

> When my kids take on issues related to race, I'm careful to avoid allowing myself to become the voice of *all* Black people—especially since I know my lived experiences impact my personal beliefs. I know I can't speak for an entire group of people. I can only speak from my position as one Black woman because our identities are complex and ever changing. Yes, I'm Black but I'm many other things at the same time.
>
> I was raised in a single-parent household in a small, rural town. I grew up poor but didn't know it. Much of who I am and what I advocate for stems from the treatment I received during my early schooling. I had countless teachers who didn't try to help me or others who looked like me reach our fullest potential. It was as if "being Black" somehow told them 100 percent of what they needed to know.
>
> While I'm sure there are Black children in my classroom who can identify with this small portion of my identity, I can't assume this is the case for them all. For some, the emotional trauma from my childhood circumstances is all too familiar. For others, this isn't relatable at all.

Navigating Complex Discussions Despite Our Cultural Blinders

To say we have prejudices and cultural blinders that make this work challenging is not to say we should shy away from the challenge. Not at all. The first step is acknowledging this work needs to be done.

A few years ago I was engaged in a discussion about social justice teaching in elementary classrooms when a kindergarten teacher raised her hand and reasoned, "I just don't think this is necessary with my babies. They *already* love each other. They don't even talk about race." A handful of others nodded in agreement. But it's not enough for kids simply to be kind to one another. Kindness fails to address the myriad of systemic injustices plaguing our society. In addition to helping our children learn the value of kindness, we need to commit ourselves to disrupting the harmful beliefs and practices that bring about such injustices. Although there are many paths to making such strides, I'm going to discuss four important steps to take on this journey: (1) take stock of your own social identities, (2) engage in discussions with a diversity of peers, (3) access texts that expand your cultural competence, and (4) engage in reflective thought.

Take Stock of Your Own Social Identities

Tool ⚒

Earlier I invited you to select one aspect of your social identity that places you within a dominant social group in our society for the purpose of identifying any unearned privileges this membership affords you. These privileges often include the fact you don't need to spend much, if any, time thinking about how this group membership affects your life. But don't stop there. To the best of your ability, make a list of *all* the social groups you belong to. Some of mine include:

Middle-aged	Raised blue-collar	Currently middle class	PhD
White	Male		English speaking
Heterosexual	Married	Able-bodied	Cisgender
U.S. born	Native Midwesterner	Father	Adoptive parent
Liberal/ independent	Formally educated	Transplant to the South	Atheist
			Educator

Like me, you'll likely find some of these place you within the dominant social group and others leave you at the margins. For instance, my identity as an atheist now living in the South definitely places me outside the dominant culture. This is a topic I think about quite often because it's not always easy for me to navigate with my classroom families. Whereas people in St. Louis (the largest metropolitan area near the small town where I grew up) often liked to ask where someone went to high school to get an initial reading of who they were and where specifically they came from, those in my current Southern community are much more likely to seek out the same information by asking where one goes to church. Because my response is sometimes accompanied by a form of judgment questioning my morality, I speak carefully but truthfully in these discussions. I see my role as helping students and their families expand their understanding of what it means to be atheist—beyond false information or stereotypes.

Not surprisingly, these experiences have provided me a particular cultural lens through which to view both religion and religious institutions—a lens not shared by many in my classroom. For this reason, I have to be aware of how I'm positioned to the topic of religion when one of my students chooses to engage us in a discussion about religious beliefs. I certainly don't want to indoctrinate my kids into obediently adopting my personal beliefs. But more than that I want to be mindful about how my social identity as an atheist, and the cultural blind spots growing out of this, potentially shape my contributions to our classroom discussions.

Engage in Discussions with a Diversity of Peers

Knowing that one of the most challenging and dangerous barriers we face is our own ignorance around a wide variety of issues, it's imperative we seek out discussions with others whose experiences are different from our own. Of course, this begins by taking a closer look at the people with whom we choose to surround ourselves. If the answer is others who are just like us in most ways, we're not apt to find ourselves in fertile discussions all that often—certainly not ones that challenge us to see the world anew. If you find your inner circle of friends is largely a reflection of your cultural self, you might begin by stepping outside this "birds of a feather flock together" tendency and form some new relationships that can provide greater richness.

Beyond a potential ignorance about particular issues, another key challenge teachers have when engaged in classroom discussions of social justice is the fact many of us have not engaged in these discussions very often ourselves—certainly, not within a diverse setting of perspectives. As such, we attempt to construct a complex structure in our classroom with very limited real-life experience to draw upon. For this reason, teachers must begin entering into genuine exploratory discussions of their own.

However, I should share one piece of advice for those entering discussions where you are positioned as a member of the dominant group. It's this: listen far more than you speak. This can be hard, listening. Yet it's crucial. There's already far too much white-splaining, man-splaining, straight-splaining, and various other forms of the dominant group attempting to draw on incomplete and misguided understandings to explain to marginalized groups what *really* happened or how they *should* feel about something.

Many times I've desperately wanted to speak so I could offer what would amount to a half-baked rationalization for a very real problem. But I've learned it's much more important to listen closely. For instance, I can remember being surprised by how much some fear the sound of a police siren. Within a discussion of abuses of power, a fellow PhD candidate of Color told of being pulled over and having the officer draw his gun, point it directly at her, and scream instructions to place her hands on the dashboard. Her perceived misstep was reaching into her purse to get her license. This experience was so visceral for her that she sobbed heavily when recounting the story. As I make sense of the hypothetical story of Mrs. Miller and the young boy wanting to understand why the police are killing unarmed Black men, I can't help but think about the image of my classmate's body shaking as she relived her encounter with a police officer who, based on his own biases about the Black community, assumed she was a potential threat. I wonder how knowing this woman's experiences as a Black woman who had stared down the lethal end of a police officer's sidearm would instruct Mrs. Miller on how best to handle her student's question about the policing of the Black community.

This is important because when I sat in that university classroom listening to my classmate's story of the police officer and the gun, I really wanted to explain it all away for her. As happens too often, it would've been easy for me to offer up excuses intended to somehow make it all OK, and then expect my perspective as a white man to be accepted as truth. Those from dominant social groups do this all the time when devaluing the lived experiences of those who've been minoritized and marginalized for centuries. For this reason, we must learn to listen more closely as we open our minds and hearts to the fact not all people experience the world as we do.

Access Texts That Expand Your Cultural Competence

Reading is another tool to expand our cultural competence. I'm defining cultural competence here as the ability to take stock of our social identities, its impact on us and others, as well as the cultural being of others. Just because you may have been the unknowing victim of a colonized education that rooted itself in the histories and stories of white America doesn't mean you have to continue to remain largely blind to the experiences, accomplishments, and issues of others. Seek out historical and political texts, biographies, memoirs, and fiction focusing on people who are markedly different from you in numerous ways. The perspectives found within these texts allow us to begin seeing the world from a more just and informed vantage point. In fact, many age-appropriate texts are available to share with your class as well so you can develop greater cultural competence alongside your students (as you'll see in later chapters).

Engage in Reflective Thought

Finally, as you engage in this work, take care to reflect on your social beliefs, assumptions, and expectations for others. To do this you might consider the following questions:

> How did these beliefs, assumptions, and expectations develop?
>
> How do (did) they shape how you read and interact with others?
>
> What role do (did) they play in establishing your larger worldview?
>
> If they have evolved over time, how did this happen?

Engaging in reflective thought not only allows you to peel away the layers of bigotry society has strapped you down with but also helps you better understand how we come to accept beliefs in the first place. When I think back to how I first began developing the earliest versions of my worldview, I see much of it came within the context of having grown up in a largely sheltered community as a child of the '80s. I grew up in a small steel mill town about half an hour from St. Louis. Short of driving into the city, which we rarely did, I was not exposed to much racial, economic, religious, or linguistic diversity. Outside a small handful of foreign exchange students in high school, we didn't have much ethnic diversity either. For this reason, much of what I learned about the world and the people in it came from television, movies, and music. I relied on media to help me make sense of the world; the characters placed before me often played into oppressive stereotypes validating the marginalization of entire populations of people. These stereotypes were blindly accepted by many in the dominant culture, including me. An example of this were the many movies and television programs reducing the diversity found in the Latinx community to no more than a collection of maids, criminals, and struggling immigrants.

If this is how some of my earliest beliefs formed, how did they shape the way I read and interacted with others? Well, for one, I unconsciously came to accept that white, male, straight, Christian, able-bodied, middle- to upper-class Americans were the model by which all others were to be judged. Not surprisingly, for the longest time I assumed this model represented the essence of what everyone across the globe aspired to become. My formal schooling did nothing to challenge this. In fact, my classwork supported this self-serving worldview. All my studies—from literature to science to history—consistently focused on the attributes and accomplishments of white, male, straight, Christian, able-bodied, middle- to upper-class Americans while turning a blind eye to most others. Given this, it shouldn't be surprising there was a time when I saw those who did not fit within this particular group as needing a "hand up" so they too could live up to such standards. This isn't to say I lacked an ability to care for all people. Rather, I felt a sense of pity for them, believing something must be holding them back from becoming all they could be. In what I hope you're beginning to see as a theme, I demonstrated an ability to love all people yet still held on to particular beliefs that were degrading and oppressive.

So, how did my beliefs evolve? By taking the very steps I'm laying out for you right now. I learned over time, with the help of many friends, colleagues, professors, and texts, to take stock of my social identity while learning more about those who experience the world differently than I do. Over time I've learned to decenter whiteness, maleness, straightness, and all the other social groupings that are granted unearned privileges. I haven't completed this journey. Truth is, I never will. But as I continue down this path in hopes of constructing a more just society, I also afford myself the opportunity to reflect on my growth in a way that helps me better understand the evolution of social beliefs and practices so I'll be prepared to meet the needs of my students as they navigate their own paths.

Watch ▶

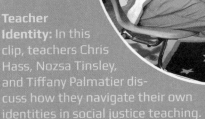

Teacher Identity: In this clip, teachers Chris Hass, Nozsa Tinsley, and Tiffany Palmatier discuss how they navigate their own identities in social justice teaching.

The Purpose and Goals of Social Justice Teaching: In this clip, Alexis, a teacher and mother of one of Chris Hass' students, talks about the purpose and goals of social justice teaching.

Classrooms That Center Social Critique

Addressing issues of social justice can be challenging work and doesn't always come naturally to many adults or young students. Yet, for Briana it did. At seven years old, she was passionate about pushing classmates to consider hard truths like the lack of representation for people of Color on sitcoms or the overrepresentation of people of Color on the nightly news (Figure 2.1). She often asked others to explain why people believed in so many hateful stereotypes and why some groups in particular seemed to think they were better or more capable than others. Though Briana lacked the historical knowledge to understand many of these injustices within a broader context, she knew they felt wrong and demanded we help her find answers.

Social critiques such as Briana's are an integral component of social justice teaching. Helping students begin to notice and name the injustices they see around them calls on us to create a new kind of classroom: one where learning no longer focuses solely on predetermined academic skills but also on efforts to better understand and disrupt systems of oppression. Yes, this can be challenging work. More often than not students are either unfamiliar with the practice of casting a critical gaze on harmful practices or they're uncomfortable sharing these concerns publicly. But, as Paulo Freire (1970) argued, we grow into the intellectual environment that surrounds us. It is up to us, then, to create such an environment. We do that by holding onto three essential elements (see Figure 2.2).

Briana: Why is it when I watch shows on Nickelodeon and Disney, there's not hardly any shows about Black kids?

Chris: Can you say more about that, Briana?

Briana: Well, when I watch Nickelodeon and Disney, I see lots of shows about white kids and white families but I don't see many Black people. So, I was wondering why there aren't really any shows about Black people. That's not right.

Alan: There are.

Briana: No, there aren't. I know because if there were, I would watch them.

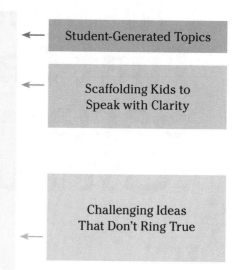

Student-Generated Topics

Scaffolding Kids to Speak with Clarity

Challenging Ideas That Don't Ring True

Figure 2.1

Second Graders Discuss Racial Representation in Children's Television

 Tool

Qualities of Student-Centered Social Justice Conversations

Student-Generated Topics: By providing our kids opportunities to pose their own questions and lead classroom discussions, we invite them into the process of creating curriculum alongside us. Their observations, questions, and concerns become an important part of our daily studies. This not only bolsters our efforts to create a culturally relevant classroom but supports our kids to build the agency they need to launch similar discussions outside the classroom.

Scaffolding Kids to Speak with Clarity: Oftentimes our kids will share ideas that are either awkwardly worded or lack needed context. In these instances we need to be careful to avoid stepping in and speaking for them. Rather, we can simply ask them to repeat their thought again or, better yet, tell us more about what they are thinking. More often than not this prompt is enough to help them speak with greater detail.

Challenging Ideas That Don't Ring True: It's important our kids learn to challenge responses that contradict their own lived experiences. In the dialogue in Figure 2.1, Alan immediately challenges Briana's claim there aren't enough shows featuring Black kids. Because as a young Black girl Briana's already paid careful attention to this troubling pattern, she is the authority and knows Alan's claim to be untrue. Alan's willingness to challenge Briana presents him with an opportunity to learn and grow as Briana is presented with an opportunity to set the record straight.

Figure 2.2

Qualities of Student-Centered Social Justice Conversations

Engaging our kids in this act of questioning and critiquing flies in the face of traditional models of education. For too long kids have felt powerless in their classrooms because they spend their days being told what to learn, how to learn it, and what to think about this all afterward. Not surprisingly, this results in a detachment between what's important to them (their experiences, interests, and concerns) and what's not (the lifeless curriculum placed in front of them). Such an approach produces students who lack the awareness, urgency, or agency required to create positive changes in their communities. We cannot allow this to continue.

It must be our daily practice to invite students into the process of creating meaning and determining what's important and why. This doesn't mean we have to restructure the whole of our curriculum or scrap all our current instructional practices. Rather, we need only to commit more time in our school day for listening and less time for talking. In doing so, we position ourselves as learners rather than sermonizers. Our job becomes to create the conditions necessary for students to genuinely explore new ideas together through open dialogue. For me, much of this dialogue happens during our Morning Meeting (as will be discussed in Chapter 6). However, it's not confined to this or any other singular classroom structure. To truly create a classroom rooted in social justice, we have to establish routines that call on us to engage our kids in social critique and action throughout the whole of the school day.

Integrated, Not Compartmentalized Social Justice Instruction

To ensure social justice work in the classroom is generative in nature and not condemned to a daily or weekly task students complete just to get to whatever comes next on the agenda, we need to be deliberate in making social justice efforts a part of *who we are* rather than just what we do. To accomplish this, social justice needs be integrated across various parts of the school day, becoming a lens through which we make sense of many of the things we learn as readers, writers, mathematicians, scientists, and social scientists. It's not enough for us to read one issue-based book each week or to occasionally set aside a half hour to talk about current events. These sorts of engagements are certainly worthwhile, but in isolation they fall short of helping our students develop a new way of being that demands they *routinely* observe the world more closely and ask critical questions.

Now, this doesn't mean we directly address issues of social justice in every single lesson. We don't. However, the potential for bringing social justice efforts into the whole of our curricular work in authentic and powerful ways is ever present. Integrating social justice into the studies we're already engaged in not only communicates the importance of this work but allows our students to take the skills they're learning in the classroom and apply them in meaningful ways. For instance, had we not stopped during a reading of Jacqueline Woodson's (2015) *Visiting Day* to notice how rarely we see stories in books about children dealing with the incarceration of a parent, Briana may not have noticed the fact there are other stories and characters missing as well. It took no more than a minute of our time during writing workshop to share an observation and then invite the kids into a brief discussion about this before returning to our writing minilesson on the use of details in powerful writing. Yet, this brief interaction was enough to inspire Briana to take notice of who is and who is not represented on her favorite television shows.

Figure 2.3

Student Drawing of Characters from Her Favorite Television Show

Representation in the Movies and Shows We Watch			
American Indians		(0)	0%
Latinx	III	(3)	5.3%
Asian-Americans	I	(1)	1.8%
African Americans	HHT III	(8)	14.3%
White	HHT HHT HHT HHT HHT HHT HHT I	(41)	73.2%
Bi-Racial	III	(3)	5.3%
		56 total	

Figure 2.4

Class Data Showing Representation on Our Favorite Television Shows

Furthermore, integrating social justice work into our everyday curriculum helps make certain this work will never be pushed aside when it feels as though there just isn't enough time in the day to get everything done. The truth is there's never going to be enough time for "yet another thing." That's why integration is key—but so are priorities. It's not enough to teach the academic skills listed in our state standards and feel as though our job is done. Nor is it enough to simply teach about issues of social justice. Our work needs to accomplish both, hand in hand. For instance, when learning to analyze different types of graphs during our math workshop, we might use this inquiry as an opportunity to study current TV listings, reflect on our own viewing habits, and generate data sets detailing patterns of representation on children's television programs as a response to Briana's concern about the lack of television shows focusing on the lives of black characters (see Figures 2.3 and 2.4). Such an engagement would provide us opportunities to meet the requirements of our state standards while critiquing social practices that have a negative impact on the identities of those outside the dominant culture. Such a simple yet purposeful engagement could lead to further academic studies, including opportunities to learn about effective public speaking and letter writing when taking action to educate others around the school or organize a letter writing campaign.

Correlating Social Justice Goals with Learning Outcomes

To integrate our social justice teaching into all parts of our curricular studies, we need to first identify what it is precisely we're integrating. Teaching Tolerance (n.d.) (https://www.tolerance.org/frameworks/social-justice-standards) developed a helpful social justice framework to organize our thinking around this work. Their framework categorizes components of social justice teaching into four distinct domains: *identity*, *diversity*, *justice*, and *activism* (see Figure 2.5 for descriptions of each). These domains do not constitute individual units or lessons that are "covered" then left behind. Rather, each moves in and out of our teaching during various parts of the school year within the context of our daily studies.

With these domains in place to guide our thinking, we're ready to begin naming the specific learning goals that will define our social justice work. The goals I've constructed for my own teaching have come as a result of many years working alongside students whose questions, ideas, and concerns have pushed my thinking to new depths.

These goals serve as a powerful guide for our work. However, they would do little good if there weren't tangible skills and strategies ascribed to each so I know *precisely* what I need to teach my students to do (or, in some cases, support them to continue doing). Figure 2.6 details the skills and strategies that are critical to achieving each goal. This chart also names the social justice domains at play when these goals and subsequent skills and strategies are put into practice. As you will notice, there are many times when a skill or strategy could easily match with more than one goal. For the sake of organization and brevity, I've chosen to include them in just one category.

Teaching Tolerance Social Justice Domains

Identity: Ensure students develop positive social identities while at the same time coming to understand their identities are complex and multilayered.

Diversity: Support students to develop a cultural competence that allows them not only to appreciate the many similarities and differences between individuals and social groups but also to understand the value these offer our society as a whole.

Justice: Teach students to recognize the relationship between individual and systemic acts of bias, injustice, and oppression, and the role power and privilege play in shaping how we experience the world.

Activism: Help students identify and dismantle their own roles in supporting harmful beliefs and practices, stand up for the rights of others, and reach out to educate others on issues that are important to them.

Figure 2.5

Teaching Tolerance Social Justice Domains

Correlation of Social Justice Goals
with Skills and Strategies

Goal	Skills and Strategies	Integrated into Practice (Social justice domains in parentheses)
Construct a strong community within the classroom.	1. Build strong relationships with a diversity of peers. 2. Show genuine interest in the lives and thoughts of others. 3. Listen to others with interest and with the intention to understand. 4. Warmly invite others into active participation to ensure they know they are welcomed and included. 5. Provide help when help is needed. 6. Acknowledge and appreciate the approximations made by others as part of the learning process. 7. Resolve conflicts in a healthy manner using respectful voices.	• Use the work of classroom discussions around literature or any other topic to teach students how to make sure all are included, genuinely heard, and respected (*identity, diversity, activism*). • Position children as both teachers and learners who support one another to grow as readers, writers, mathematicians, scientists, and social scientists (*activism*).
Appreciate the value of students' individuality as well as the many social groups to which they belong.	1. Develop a positive sense of identity as an individual as well as a member of the various social groups to which one belongs. 2. Demonstrate comfort and pride in being different from others while at the same time appreciating the similarities that bind us together.	• Make deliberate book choices that highlight the value of individuality as well as membership within multiple social groups (*identity, diversity*). • When developing critical questions for kids to discuss within various studies, include open-ended questions about how difference is taken up by characters in the book (*justice*).
Understand diversity takes on many forms and holds great value.	1. Understand our identities are not singular but the intersection of many social groups to which we belong, and that there are many similarities/differences between social groups as well as individuals within those social groups. 2. Develop a deeper understanding of other cultures that moves beyond superficial understandings and challenges stereotypes. 3. Develop an appreciation for the cultural values and contributions of various groups within the community, nation, and world.	• Make book choices that include a wide variety of characters (*identity, diversity*). • Select books that show the complexity of a character's being (*identity, diversity*). • Select a diversity of authors to highlight during author and genre studies (*identity, diversity*). • As part of typical discussions around literature, highlight those characters who defy stereotypes and demonstrate the complexity of each person and each social group (*identity, diversity*).

Correlation of Social Justice Goals with Skills and Strategies

Goal	Skills and Strategies	Integrated into Practice (*Social justice domains in parentheses*)
Possess a critical curiosity about the world.	1. Observe the world closely and ask questions about those things that seem to lack explanation. 2. Demonstrate an expectation to understand.	• Make it a common practice to stop throughout when reading a book and ask, "What are you wondering about right now?" Select issues-based texts that lead such questions to hit upon issues of social justice as well as curricular topics under study (*justice*). • During the course of literature discussions, work to get at the root of why a character may have acted in a certain way—identifying the roles of power, perspective, desires, and so on (*justice*).
Question social beliefs and practices on a regular basis.	1. Observe the world closely and ask questions about those things that seem to lack examination or justice. 2. Make connections between multiple issues and events while acknowledging the roles of power and privilege. 3. Identify our own role in supporting problematic and harmful beliefs and practices.	• Relate the questions students generate from their reading to issues within the classroom, school, and broader communities, while identifying our own role in maintaining or disrupting any injustices (*justice*). • As part of literature discussions around other topics, connect issues in fictional stories to real oppressions experienced throughout history and in the present (*justice*).
Be informed of current events and issues affecting our communities.	1. Read, analyze, and share out news articles detailing current events that speak to the rights, accomplishments, and lived experiences of those in our community, nation, and world.	• Incorporate nonfiction texts such as current news articles into the reading workshop (*identity, diversity, justice*). • Select issue-based books when in need of a text for a given minilesson, engagement, or read-aloud (*justice*).
Identify acts of oppression and the false beliefs that encourage people to support these acts.	1. Identify aspects of society that are unfair to particular social groups. 2. Name the beliefs being employed to make those in power feel just in their actions.	• When students bring attention to unjust social actions, challenge them to name potential beliefs those in power may hold and question the source of these beliefs (*justice*).

(continues)

Correlation of Social Justice Goals
with Skills and Strategies

Goal	Skills and Strategies	Integrated into Practice (Social justice domains in parentheses)
Understand the value of multiple perspectives.	1. Seek out competing understandings and weigh these against the known facts. 2. Work to understand where competing understandings come from and the beliefs on which they are constructed. 3. Seek out primary resources, including firsthand reports from those with personal experiences and knowledge. 4. Work to generate beliefs through the process of inquiry.	• Use shared texts as an opportunity to explore how different people may view the same event or issue from multiple perspectives (*diversity, justice*).
Live alongside others in a democratic way.	1. Share concerns openly and with respect for others. 2. Resolve issues and conflicts in a manner that, as much as possible, meets the needs of all involved. 3. Engage in respectful, but contested, discussion around a wide variety of topics and issues.	• Create a space where students become increasingly comfortable sharing their vulnerabilities and asking for help from others when needed (*identity, activism*). • Work collaboratively to identify issues that are hindering classroom learning and healthy relationships among peers, and develop potential solutions for these that call upon the insights and efforts of all (*justice, activism*).
Become critical consumers of information.	1. Ask where this information originated. 2. Ask for whom this information speaks. 3. Ask who this information benefits. 4. Ask who this information ignores or misrepresents.	• Teach students to interrogate texts in regard to the perspective being shared, who the story/information benefits, and who the story/information ignores or misrepresents (*justice, activism*).

Correlation of Social Justice Goals with Skills and Strategies

Goal	Skills and Strategies	Integrated into Practice (Social justice domains in parentheses)
Take action on our convictions.	1. Revise our own social beliefs and practices when they pose harm to others or support systems of oppression. 2. Disrupt acts of oppression and the false beliefs that encourage people to support these acts. 3. Identify and act upon opportunities to take our knowledge to new audiences who are in a position to create greater change.	• When identifying issues in the classroom, school, or broader community, call on students to identify actions we can take on the personal level or on a larger scale to address these issues (*justice, activism*).

Figure 2.6

Correlation of Social Justice Goals with Skills and Strategies

Student-Centered Instruction in Action

Earlier this year I had a copy of *William's Doll* (Zolotow 1972) sitting on my board tray in preparation for a minilesson I had planned for the next day. This book tells the story of a young boy who badly wants a doll but his request is met with demoralizing laughter, ridicule, and disbelief by the males in his life. One afternoon a parent came into our classroom to pick up her daughter. As the two of them were about to head out the door her daughter, Kendall, looked over and noticed the book for the first time.

"*William's Doll*?" Kendall exclaimed. "A *boy* has a doll!"

She began laughing and others around her quickly joined in. Without hesitation, her mother spoke up.

"And *what* is wrong with a boy wanting a doll?" her mother demanded. The sharp tone of her voice communicated the fact this was not so much a question but a reprimand.

Instantly, the room fell into an uncomfortable silence. Kendall—caught off guard by the public admonishment—looked down at her feet in embarrassment.

"Kendall," her mother said, in a softer voice. "What is wrong with a boy having a doll?"

"Nothing," Kendall responded obediently, lifting her gaze back up to her mother.

"That's right."

This brief ten-second episode stuck with me for some time. I kept thinking about the exchange between Kendall and her mother in relation to indoctrination and the construction of new beliefs. Kendall's mother worked swiftly and coercively to ensure her daughter understood it was wrong to laugh at a boy for wanting a doll. As parents, we take similar actions all the time. We do the same as teachers—demanding our students wait patiently for their turn, preaching the value of always doing their best, and insisting they treat others with kindness and respect. We're forever teaching our children to adopt our own morals. But is this form of socializing our children the most valuable method for gaining *all* knowledge in the social justice classroom? Not really.

How we choose to respond to the problematic social beliefs and practices our children demonstrate depends a lot on the particulars of the situation as well as our goals for them as learners and citizens. Yet, how our students go about establishing beliefs in the classrooms is incredibly important because this process of learning will serve as a model for the critical thinking skills they're likely to embrace in their lives outside the classroom. If one of our goals is to help students become critical thinkers who scrutinize the unjust beliefs and practices of this society, we want to make sure our classroom practices are aligned with this goal. We cannot fall into the trap of preaching from on high. To do so is shortsighted.

 Tool

Framework for Evaluating Beliefs

One of my favorite topics to explore with my students is how people come to believe things are true—especially when these bits of information are altogether false. To understand this, I draw on nineteenth-century philosopher Charles Peirce. Peirce (1877) argued there are four ways through which a person forms a belief: (1) authority, (2) a priori, (3) tenacity, and (4) inquiry. The first three of these forms are unscientific and unreliable, yet that doesn't mean they aren't the primary foundation for many things we believe to be fact. Only by learning to unpack these forms through inquiry can we arrive at some meaningful truth.

Authority: "I was told by someone I trust."

The first method of fixating belief is through *authority*. Establishing a new belief by means of authority takes the form of a trusted figure telling us something is true and, by virtue of their status in relation to our own, adopting their truth as our own. A few years ago, during the 2016 presidential campaign, one of my students openly questioned why Donald Trump wanted to build a wall between the United States and Mexico. This student suggested such an act might make Donald Trump racist since he'd also talked negatively about the people who come to the United States from

Mexico. Another student in class, Peter, quickly defended Trump, responding "He's not racist—he just wants to keep us safe."

When asked what the wall would keep us safe *from* and how he knew these dangers existed, Peter couldn't respond. Rather, his beliefs that a border wall would be just, that it would protect us, and that Mexican citizens passing over the border illegally were dangerous had likely been formed through authority—perhaps by a family member, a friend, or a piece of a story he overheard on the news. Yet, until this moment these beliefs had gone unchallenged. This is the danger of fixating belief through authority. When we look to parents, teachers, clergy, counselors, or friends, we often prevent ourselves from fully understanding or even questioning the information we receive.

That said, there is much to know in this world and we cannot be experts on everything. Nor do we have the time to research all of these things for ourselves. So, we make choices as to when to rely on others for information and when to work out this information for ourselves. In either case, it's good practice to always scrutinize new information received from those in a position of authority rather than blindly to accept it as truth.

A Priori: "It just sounds right to me."

Another method of fixating belief is *a priori*. A priori knowledge speaks to the notion that if you just think hard enough, even when lacking adequate experience to draw upon, you can independently come to a truth—as though this truth is somewhere in the air just waiting to be plucked down. Certainly, there have been instances of scientific study when a sort of blind logic has led to a scientific hypothesis that was later confirmed to be true. However, in the social world this can be dangerous, because a priori knowledge often takes the form of "It just sounds right to me." This, in turn, can be self-serving as people tend to want to believe those things that feel most comfortable to them or that benefit them in some way.

For example, two girls in my class once returned from PE upset over the fact they'd just completed a stamina assessment where the boys' standard of achievement was set higher than the girls. Exasperated, the girls shared their frustration as we tried to settle in for our literacy workshop. Hearing their complaints, a few of the boys attempted to rationalize the fact fewer laps were expected of the girls by introducing beliefs they'd likely established through blind logic. The boys argued girls are less athletic and less fit, thus are assigned lower expectations. These boys had no hard facts and very few experiences to support their claims. In fact, many of the girls in class had outperformed the boys on the day's assessment and the top score in the entire school belonged to an older sister of one of them. Though these firsthand experiences should have told the students otherwise, they still relied on their own logic to help them justify the PE teacher's expectations.

Tenacity: "This fits with what I've always believed."

The third form of fixating belief is referred to as *tenacity*. Tenacity refers to our willingness and desire to hold steady to beliefs no matter what new information may be presented to us. Because the beliefs we already hold can often serve as our gold standard for truth, there are many times when we vehemently reject new information because it brings into question or altogether disproves those beliefs we already hold so dear. As such, we tend to believe new things simply because they fit within the framework of already existing beliefs. My small group of boys in class demonstrated this when refusing to consider the fact the girls, as a whole, had outperformed them on the PE assessment or the fact there were more girls in this particular class who played organized sports than boys. The idea that girls could be more fit or more athletic did not conform with their worldview, so they chose to pay attention only to those things that allowed them to maintain their current beliefs.

Inquiry: "I need to work hard to make sure this is true."

The final form of fixating belief presented by Peirce (1877) is the *scientific method*, or what I will refer to within the context of our work around social justice as *inquiry* (Mills 2014). Inquiry in the social justice classroom refers to our ability to observe the world closely, ask questions about those things that lack order or justice, consider information gleaned from reliable sources, and interrogate our developing understandings with a diverse group of thinkers willing to push us to consider diverse perspectives. The girls returning from the stamina assessment in PE provided us a perfect opportunity for such inquiry. Their willingness to openly question previously unchallenged gendered beliefs and practices in the PE classroom created an opportunity for each of us to question where these expectations came from, whether or not they were fair or accurate, and what potential for harm they posed. The privilege of higher expectations granted to boys in PE was brought into focus as information about individual student performance was carefully considered and multiple perspectives were shared. If it were not for the process of rich discussion aimed at disrupting the convenience of authority, a priori, and tenacity, my small group of boys, who wanted so badly to hold firm to the belief they deserved higher expectations no matter their personal level of fitness, would not have had an opportunity to learn their female counterparts experienced the PE classroom much differently than they did.

Setting Our Expectations

On paper, the work of examining our beliefs through inquiry all seems simple enough. Yet, our experiences in the classroom tell us it's rarely easy. Every student's path to new learning is unique and, many times, fraught with obstacles along the way.

A few years ago one of my students, Elena, noticed that some in the class talked a big game when discussing social justice yet fell short of actually living into these ideals in their daily actions. She brought this to our attention during Morning Meeting.

Elena: I was wondering why we say one thing in Morning Meeting but then act a different way later.

Chris: What do you mean?

Elena: It's just like we say stuff at Morning Meeting about being nice to other people but then we don't really do that. Not usually.

Chris: Not usually or not always?

Elena: Well, not always. But everyone acts like they're worried about doing the right thing when we talk in here.

Peter: Yeah, I've seen that too. Like I see people teasing or saying people are weird . . . I remember when you showed us that book of people from around the world and some people said "Ew" when you got to the page where they were wearing just a little clothes and had tattoos or something.

Kumail: I don't think people really believe what they say in Morning Meeting because they don't do it. They don't do the things they say.

Chris: So, it seems like there's a breakdown between our beliefs, how we say the world *should* be, and our actions when we leave Morning Meeting. What do you all think about this? What might make us say things should be a certain way but then go out and do the exact opposite sometimes?

Elena's concern was a fair one. When we know better, we should do better. We spend months celebrating the richness of our kids' contributions to the classroom and to their communities (*identity*). We develop curriculum to help them better understand the complexity and brilliance of a world where not everyone is the same (*diversity*). We implement classroom structures to ensure they're prepared to observe the world more carefully and think critically about those things that appear unfair (*justice*). Yet, without a commitment to the final domain of social justice teaching, *action*, it can feel as though we're doing little more than just spinning our wheels.

We expect to see our kids working to actively transform their world for the better—beginning with themselves. But sometimes this transformation isn't as evident as we'd like. We shouldn't be surprised. Learning is a journey, not a race. Just as with any other part of our curriculum, our kids need a steady supply of authentic experiences and plenty of time to process in the company of others. That's how learning works. Although Elena's concern may have been fair, her expectation for immediate change was not. Transformation is a complicated process. Much of what we're trying to change is so deeply woven into the fabric of our being we aren't even aware of its presence. I'll give you an example.

One day I pulled out Eve Bunting's book *One Green Apple* (2006) to read aloud as part of an inquiry into making inferences. This beautiful book tells the story of a young girl, Farah, who recently immigrated to the United States. On a field trip to the apple orchard, Farah feels isolated from her new world because everything seems so different. However, in time she comes to recognize a sense of familiarity in many of the things she sees and hears.

The cover of the book features olive-skinned Farah smiling contentedly while holding a small green apple in her cupped hands. She's dressed in a white T-shirt and a hijab that loosely frames her face. I asked, "Based on the title and the illustration, what do you think this book is going to be about?" This is a question I often ask before reading a book aloud. It helps prepare my kids for the story ahead while also providing me a glimpse into their thinking. Although many guessed the story would have something to do with a girl going to an apple orchard to pick apples, a few others created an entirely different meaning from the illustration.

Alan: I think it's going to be about a girl who's poor.

Chris: What do you mean, what makes you think that?

Alan: Well, the girl on the cover looks like she's poor.

Jaylen: Yeah, I was going to say that, too.

Chris: What is it about the illustration that makes you think she's poor?

Alan: Uh, I don't know. I just think she is. Where is she from?

Laila: That doesn't make any sense, Alan. She does not look poor.

Chris: Hmm, what does it mean to *look* poor? I don't know this is something you can always see.

Jaylen: Well she might be poor. She might be smiling to have the apple because she was hungry because she didn't have enough food. Maybe they don't have enough food where she is.

Laila: What? Where do you think she is? I don't think you . . .

Caitlin: I think she's in America. The kids behind her look white. But I don't think she's poor. I think that might be a stereotype.

Alan and Jaylen both assumed, based on Farah's appearance, she must be from somewhere other than America and that she must be poor. Given all the work we'd done together to have a greater understanding of diversity and to discredit stereotypes, how could this be? The truth is, our beliefs are often ahead of our practices (Mills 2015). Just because Alan and Jaylen knew what beliefs they wanted to live into (in this case, resisting deficit-based thinking about social groups other than their own) didn't mean they were prepared, just yet, to hit this mark in their daily practices. For one, they hadn't had nearly enough time to take stock of the many stereotypes they'd unknowingly accepted as truth. The countless messages Alan and Jaylen had received about difference over the course of their lives weren't going to be undone by a single class discussion or even a series of class discussions. It just doesn't work that way.

So, let's not base our expectations for students *solely* on the short-term product of this work. Although we most certainly want to see every single one of our children peel away the harmful beliefs and assumptions they've developed over the course of their short lives, it cannot serve as the *only* measure of growth. Rather, we need to provide greater balance in our expectations by also acknowledging the stance they take as learners engaged in social justice work.

Watch ▶

Connecting History to Contemporary Media: In this clip, second grader Brooklyn explains the topic of her persuasive writing piece for social studies. Negative responses to a biracial family in a Cheerios commercial led her to write about how slavery's legacy is not over in the United States.

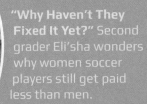

"Why Haven't They Fixed It Yet?" Second grader Eli'sha wonders why women soccer players still get paid less than men.

Identity
Knowing Our Students

A number of years ago I asked my kids to read back through their memory story drafts and identify a single sentence they felt burned with incredible importance. "It should be a sentence that really says a lot about you or helps us understand why this story is so significant," I explained. They took a few moments selecting their passages and then wrote about them. Afterward, I asked if anyone wanted to share out to the whole group. The usual hands shot into the air. Some had written about their love of sports, others spoke to their affection for animals, and one or two comically told stories about constant arguments with their siblings.

Just when I thought no one else wanted to share out, an unexpected hand slowly raised into the air. It was Colby, a new student who'd joined our class just a few weeks before. Colby was a bit shy and had yet to form relationships with his new classmates. Despite a number of efforts, we still didn't know much about him. Colby nervously walked to the front of the group, took a seat, and explained, "My sentence was, *My bedroom was mostly empty.*" He began:

> I chose [this sentence] because I don't have nothing in my room. Just a bed and a dresser. I have clothes but there's no toys or nothing.

Colby went on to explain his parents had recently separated and he and his mom were temporarily living at his grandmother's house. They didn't have all their things from the old house and he felt as though his life had been turned upside down. After Colby finished, there was an incredible stillness in the room as each of us sat not only absorbing the details of what we'd just learned but surprised by his willingness to share it so openly with us. Eventually a couple kids raised their hands to agree these changes were hard. Someone else told him his room was probably really cool even if there weren't many toys.

I thanked Colby for bravely sharing such a personal piece of his life with us and reminded him how grateful we were to have him as part of our classroom family.

Over time Colby shared more and more details about his life outside of school. These rich layers of his life revealed themselves, primarily, during Morning Meeting discussions and class transitions and in response to the many picture books we read together. We learned about Colby's love of hunting, his close relationship with his uncle, and his desire to have a pet of his own—preferably a dog. As was the case with each of his classmates, Colby's life experiences included many celebrations but a few hardships too. These experiences not only shaped how he viewed the world but played a powerful role in molding the image he'd come to develop of himself as a person and a learner.

Too often, we fail to recognize the significance of these moments when our students share themselves with us—times when we're offered an opportunity to peek into the inner lives of our kids and know them as more than just readers, writers, scientists, social scientists, and mathematicians. When I look back on my own schooling experiences as a student, I'm hard-pressed to think of many teachers who knew a single thing about me outside my test scores or my willingness to comply with classroom rules. I was, in essence, just another student. I can't help but think this played a significant role in my disengagement as a student for the bulk of my schooling.

Most would agree it's important to get to know our students. Yet, knowing precisely what to do with the information we glean allows us to move beyond the limitations of being well intentioned to a place where our deliberate and well-informed choices allow us to develop socially just practices in our classrooms. In this chapter I explore the potential of knowing our kids.

Inquiring into Our Students' Social Identities

One of the challenges facing Colby was the fact he didn't feel he fit in with the other kids. Worse, he felt inferior. One day at recess I asked him how he felt his relationships with the other kids were developing. At first he said everything was OK, but as our discussion continued he slowly admitted he didn't think the other kids really wanted to be his friend. They were nice to him, yes, but they rarely invited him to join their games and no one had ever asked him to be their partner or to eat together at lunch. I asked him why this might be and he said he thought he was different from the other kids. He worried he was too unathletic to fit in with the boys and felt like he had even less in common with the girls. He also worried about "all the problems" his family was having. I took this to mean he felt like his current family structure (estranged father), living situation (loss of home), and socioeconomic status (unemployed mother) made him feel inadequate in relation to the assumptions he was making about the home lives of his classmates.

Stories such as Colby's serve as powerful demonstrations of the need for teachers to ensure students develop and maintain positive social identities. In particular, children from marginalized groups are often made to feel some level of inferiority based on their gender, ethnicity, race, religion, physical ability, socioeconomic status, or a host of other social factors. Our kids should learn to take pride in the particulars of who they are no matter the struggles they or their families might be facing in the present. Furthermore, it's important to note that even students who enjoy great levels of acceptance by their peers require these same considerations. This is because although nondominant aspects of their identities might be celebrated within their small classroom community (say, their Mexican heritage), these same social identities will be challenged in other spaces (such as politicians playing upon oppressive stereotypes of Mexicans while discussing proposed immigration reform). For this reason, it's our duty to help our students celebrate all that connects them to others as well as sets them apart. There are specific steps we can take to do this, each growing out of an underlying principle about the relationship between classroom engagements and identity (see Figure 3.1).

Building and Maintaining Positive Social Identities — Tool

Underlying Principle	Classroom Practice
It is essential to normalize and celebrate the diversity found within our communities.	We choose and make available in the classroom books that provide consistent opportunities for our kids to see themselves reflected in the books we share.
The story of America students learn is often used to reinforce the power of white males.	We intentionally disrupt the centering of whiteness and maleness by sharing current and historical accounts depicting the lives and accomplishments of diverse and under-represented groups of people.
The cultural practice and knowledge present in each of our student's homes have great value.	We invite our kids' family members and guardians to share aspects of their home culture and interests with our class.
Students learn best when given opportunities to make explicit connections between classroom learning and their personal lives.	We create authentic opportunities for our kids to share pieces of their personal lives with us through writing, responses to literature, and classroom discussion.

Figure 3.1
Building and Maintaining Positive Social Identities

Selecting Literature That Reflects the Social Identities of Our Students

One way to help students develop and maintain positive social identities is to make certain our classroom books reflect the many components of their identities. Of course, we can't be sure we're hitting this mark unless we've taken the time to really get to know our kids as individuals. This may begin with the more visible aspects of their identities but it can't stop there. Yes, we need books featuring characters who are Black, Latinx, Asian American, mixed race, and so on, but our kids' identities extend far beyond their ethnic heritage or racial makeup. Other factors such as family structure, religion, socioeconomic status, health, gender identification, interests, and abilities need to be taken into account as well. Remember, none of us can be defined by a single aspect of our identities; rather, we exist at the intersection of the many social groups to which we belong.

Celebrating the Contributions of All

Second, we can make certain the news articles and historical accounts we share in the classroom reflect a diversity of populations. Our kids need to hear the accounts of people from both the present and the past, such as César Chávez, Malala Yousafzai, Harvey Milk, Marian Wright Edelman, and so many others whose stories show the impact all communities of people have made to create a better and more just world for us all. When classrooms continue to narrowly define what counts as relevant (namely, the contributions made by white, upper- to middle-class, straight, physically abled, Christian men), they not only turn a blind eye to the many contributions made by those from marginalized communities but also become part of a larger system of oppression that acts to normalize the dominance of those in power.

Inviting Family Members into the Class to Share

The third way we can bolster our kids' social identities is to invite family members into the classroom to share parts of their home cultures, interests, and areas of expertise with us. Few things hold more power than having a guest from home join the class to share pieces of their lives. From a brief introduction to languages spoken at home to descriptions of important family traditions, there are an infinite number of possibilities. For valid reasons, some families and caregivers will not be able or willing to come into the classroom. However, in these cases we can still invite them to send a note or artifact their child can share with the class. In any case, it's our responsibility to do everything possible to ensure our kids have ample opportunities to share their home lives with us.

Using Curriculum to Draw Out Personal Stories

Last, as was the case when Colby told us about his troubles at home, we can carve out opportunities for our students to share pieces of themselves with us through writing, responses to reading, and classroom discussions. This becomes possible when we provide open invitations to our kids to make connections between their home lives and the work we're doing in the classroom. For instance, we can set aside time for students to share out special moments or announcements during our Morning Meeting. Or we can get into the regular practice of stopping after a particularly engaging passage in a book and asking, "Who has a connection to this?" In doing this work, we offer our kids opportunities both to share and celebrate all that makes them who they are.

Inquiring into Our Students' Funds of Knowledge

Another challenge facing Colby was that he felt a disconnect between schooling and his personal life. When Colby joined us, he wasn't a particularly invested learner. Conversations with his mother helped me understand he had a history of doing just enough to stay out of trouble but had never really devoted himself to learning. She said Colby was bored and oftentimes frustrated by school. Sure enough, when independent reading time rolled around, Colby would randomly grab a book from the shelf and aimlessly rifle through it until he was told he could stop. In writing workshop he'd start a number of pieces only to later abandon them. During math he'd take a stab at a few problems, wrinkle his forehead, and then start doodling at the margins of his paper.

So, how *can* we reach students like Colby who feel disengaged or uninterested as learners? First, we can work from the understanding that all students learn best when classroom content is culturally relevant to their personal lives (Howard 2010). Learning becomes easier when the specifics of what we're learning is placed within familiar contexts. Second, we can ensure all new learning builds on the knowledge our kids have already acquired in their homes and communities. Geneva Gay (2010) writes:

> **Virtually every student can do something well. Even if students' capabilities are not directly translatable to classroom learning, they still can be used by teachers as points of reference and motivational devices to evoke student interest and involvement in academic affairs. Teachers must learn how to recognize, honor, and incorporate the personal abilities of students into their teaching strategies. If this is done, then school achievement will improve. (1)**

To get to know our students well means allowing them to teach us about their interests, talents, and desires. All of these have the potential to become springboards to new learning as well as guide our selection of classroom resources. Working with Colby, I knew he particularly loved to go fishing with his uncle. Over the course of the year these became the stories he loved to tell most. He also knew a great deal about cars. These two pieces of information, in addition other data I collected about him, allowed me to help him in the following ways:

- I located reading materials I felt were more likely to engage him as a reader. Due to their familiar content, these books also increased his likelihood of understanding the text.

- I helped Colby generate lists of interests and strong memories to fuel his writing. The ideas he jotted in the back of his writing journal were far more engaging and purposeful than those he initially attempted after joining our class, thus dramatically improving the likelihood he'd be invested in his writing.

- I helped Colby better understand key mathematical skills and strategies (i.e., word problems, repeated addition, fractions) by placing them within familiar contexts based on his interests and previous knowledge. For instance, he and I worked together to create word problems about fish populations in South Carolina lakes or the differences in horsepower between various powerful engines.

Although connecting Colby's classroom learning to his interests and funds of knowledge allowed him to engage more deeply with our content and find improved success, it was not a panacea. Kids are complicated and so, too, is schooling—especially given limitations in staff and resources at many schools. In truth, Colby oftentimes needed more academic support than I could provide him given the fact I had many other students who needed me as well. I share this because I don't want to oversimplify how complex the acts of teaching and learning are. That said, we do our students a great service when we make deliberate efforts to incorporate what we know about them into our classroom practices. As Geneva Gay (2010) explained, when teaching and learning are culturally relevant to our students' lives, they *will* achieve better.

Developing Intentional Practices to Better Know Our Kids

When we make it our mission to help students build positive social identities as well as ensure our curriculum is culturally relevant to the particulars of their lives, we must first put in the work of getting to know them really well. But what does this look like? A great place to begin is by simply carving out as much time as possible to sit and talk with our kids. Time spent hanging out together at the lunch table, playing at recess, or tidying up together after school is time well spent. Though schedules and duties differ from classroom to classroom, there's always time available somewhere in the day to sit and swap stories. In this same vein, another great option is to start a discussion journal with each of your students where you write letters back and forth or have written conversations. I first learned about written conversations (Burke, Harste, and Short 1998) from my colleague and mentor, Tim O'Keefe. Each year Tim dedicated a part of his reading and writing conference time to conversing back and forth with his kids on paper (see Figure 3.2). Written conversations are a great literacy practice designed to scaffold students into more conventional writing practices. However, as Tim demonstrated through his practice, these collaborative documents also provide a rich opportunity to inquire into our kids' families, communities, interests, hopes, fears, successes, struggles, and aspirations. There are great amounts of information to be mined if only we invest the time and effort.

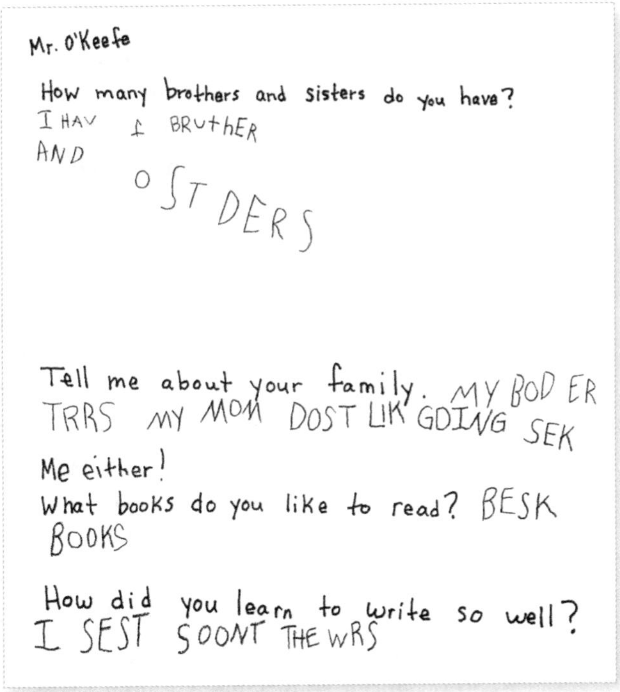

Mr. O'Keefe

How many brothers and sisters do you have? I HAV 1 BRUTHER AND 0 STDERS

Tell me about your family. MY BODER TRRS MY MOM DOST LIK GOING SEK

Me either!

What books do you like to read? BESK BOOKS

How did you learn to write so well? I SEST SOONT THE WRS

Figure 3.2
Written Conversation with a Kindergartner

There are also a number of formal practices and inquiries we can put into place to efficiently and effectively get to know our students better. Although the possibilities for such work are limitless, I'm going to present three in particular that hold great potential and make for a powerful place to begin this journey. These include (1) inquiries into the histories of our names, (2) intake conferences, and (3) family book recommendations.

Inquiring into the Histories of Our Names

My oldest son, Muluken, was born in Ethiopia. From his first days in America as a six-year-old, it was clear his name was a challenge for many Americans to pronounce. In truth, it's not that difficult to say: *Muh–LUE–ken.* You need only to listen to it carefully and then commit to getting it right. It takes five or ten seconds, tops. However, not everyone who's passed through his life has been willing to invest those few moments. As a result, his name gets mangled on a regular basis. It was once even suggested to him by a high school teacher that he shorten his name to Luke to avoid future mispronunciations. As educators dedicated to social justice, we know continually pronouncing our kids' names incorrectly or changing them for our own convenience is not only culturally insensitive but highly offensive. Our names are important. Muluken's name connects him to the country that will forever be a significant part of his identity (Ethiopia) as well as the important person that gave it to him—his birth mother.

Because the origins of our names often have stories that can be powerful, informative, or fun, early in the school year I like to invite my students to go home and find out more about the history of their names. To set this engagement up for success, my kids and I work together to decide what questions we want answered (see Figure 3.3). As with so much of our learning, I know it's important to invite students into the process of creating curriculum. To support engagement as well as relevance to their lives, I need to find out what they'd like to learn in addition to the things I already know we'll need to uncover. I mention this because we're continually at risk of missing out on meaningful experiences with our students when the work we give them feels more like task completion ("Go home and have your parents help you fill out this questionnaire") than a genuine exploration ("What would you *really* like to know about your name?"). Their ideas are often quite rich.

Maya: I'd like to know who came up with my name.

Chris: Do you know already?

Maya: I think my mom probably. But maybe my dad. He loves my name.

William: I'm named after my great, great Grandpop.

Chris: That's so cool! OK, so there's two things: who came up with your name and where did it come from? I know when my wife and I named our kids, we kept suggesting names back and forth. Some we agreed on and some we didn't at all. Some had a special importance to us and others we just liked the way they sounded. What else? What would you like to know about the origins of your name?

Tiffany: Maybe . . . why they picked it?

Chris: What do you mean?

Tiffany: Like, why they picked that name and not another one.

Chris: OK, so maybe why that particular name felt so important?

Tiffany: Yeah.

My goals for this engagement are threefold. First, I want to make it clear very early on to both my students and their families that I'm interested in their lives and their stories. Of course, this doesn't happen simply by having the kids bring home a worksheet to fill out. Rather, communicating my investment comes from actually doing something of importance with the information gleaned from their responses. To build a relationship of trust, I know making something of what I learn about them is key. One way I accomplish this is to have the kids write and present a short piece teaching the rest of us about their names. In addition to giving value to each of our names, stories, and home cultures, this is also a wonderful opportunity for the kids to learn the importance of listening *patiently* and listening *actively* to the stories of others (Kay 2018). As will be discussed later, helping young students learn to pay careful attention to the ideas and stories of others is a critical skill that pays huge dividends over the course of an entire year in the social justice classroom.

Figure 3.3

Collection of Kids' Ideas for Name Inquiry

My second goal for this project is to begin acquiring artifacts to fill our room that reflect who we are. In my earliest days of teaching I filled the classroom walls with posters and other instructional materials well before my kids appeared for the first day of school. Knowing better, I no longer do this. Now I wait and let them help me fill these spaces with genuine pieces we create together. Just as the artifacts in museums should reflect the many communities they serve, so should the artifacts in our classrooms. To achieve this, we display our name pieces in a prominent space on the classroom walls and invite classroom guests, including our families, to spend time learning about their origins and meanings.

My third goal for this project is to help me learn about my kids' families. Naming a child is a big task, and the decisions we make can often times reveal a lot about us. For instance, Pierce's family named him after a former college baseball player from the local university. His parents appreciated that his name would be unique and reflect their family's love of baseball. Not surprisingly, much of Pierce's time is spent on the ball field as he travels on the weekends for tournaments around the state. Maya, on the other hand, was proud that her name could be found "all over the world." Forever interested in learning about other people and cultures, she enjoyed traveling to Israel to spend time with members of her family—particularly her grandmother who, she proudly told us, had "survived the Holocaust!" As you can imagine, the depth of this information doesn't always make it into the paragraphs my seven-year-old students write for me during that second week of school. Nor does it often make it into the short presentations they give their classmates. However, what *is* there gives me just enough information to guide future conversations with their parents when they stop by to drop something off. It also helps feed the discussions I have with my kids as we eat our lunches together in the cafeteria or hang out at recess. In this way, their name projects offer me an entry point for my yearlong inquiry into their lives.

Intake Conferences

Another great way to learn more about our students is to turn the traditional parent–teacher conference on its head by asking our classroom families to come in and teach us about their children. I first learned about this practice more than twenty years ago when I began my teaching career at the New City School in St. Louis. Committed to responsive teaching practices, the school's faculty and administration established this as a valued whole-school structure. Fittingly, these conferences positioned parents and caregivers as the experts while teachers, poised to learn, attentively collected information that would be key to establishing strong home–school relationships as well as informing classroom practices. Those families who couldn't make it into school were offered opportunities to speak by telephone. Over the years I've drawn upon many of the questions used at New City School and added others that meet my particular needs (see Figure 3.4). As you can imagine, the conversations that grow

 Tool

Intake Conference Questions

1. Tell me about your child. What would you like for me to know?
2. What are your child's interests? What do they love to do most?
3. Is your child involved in activities outside of school? If so, what does this look like on a nightly/weekly basis?
4. Are there any religious, cultural, or ethnic holidays, observances, or traditions that are important to your family? Will any of these affect your child's participation at school? Are you willing to come in and share any of these with our class?
5. What does your family love to do together?
6. Can you tell me a little about your child's friendships?
7. How does your child view school? What do you attribute this to?
8. Thinking of academics, what tends to come most easily for your child? Is there anything that's been especially challenging up to this point?
9. How do you navigate any work that might come home from time to time? Is there a routine? Do you help your child with this or is there an expectation they do it independently?
10. What are your goals for your child this year?

Figure 3.4
Intake Conference Questions

out of these questions provide a rich opportunity to learn about a child's interests, family traditions, successes, tensions, friendships, nightly schedules, learning histories, attitudes toward schooling, and more.

Many teachers already carve out time for similar conversations with families. Some even take this work a step further by scheduling home visits. There could be no better investment of our time than sitting in the company of our kids' families and offering them our full attention. That said, I've had years where special circumstances made it incredibly difficult to fit in conferences with twenty-plus families—especially given the fact my own children were at home waiting to spend time with me as well. Given these limitations, some teachers choose to send questionnaires home with their students during the first week or two of school. Although not as powerful as a face-to-face conference or a home visit, written responses are still capable of providing important information to guide our instruction, shape our resources, and feed future conversations with our kids and their families.

Family Book Recommendations

One of my favorite examples of inviting families to share information (and one I've stolen for my own use) comes from my colleague, Tiffany Palmatier. Tiffany teaches kindergarten and first grade, looping up with each group. During their kindergarten year, Tiffany launches a literature study where she asks her classroom families to send in or suggest a book title capturing some aspect of their child's identity (see Figure 3.5). Tiffany understands the need to not only get to know her students better but also to begin establishing trust with families by opening up lines of communication between school and home.

Upcoming Family Recommendation Literature Study

Teach young people early on that in diversity there is
beauty and there is strength.   —Maya Angelou

*I am so excited about the Family Recommendation Literature (picture book)
Study taking place during the month of October. I plan to read my personal favorite (I Like Myself) to the kiddos next week. When I found the book years ago, I
was so drawn to the beautiful illustrations. I felt like I could relate to the story in
so many different ways! The main character's hair looks like mine when I wash
it, and the book conveys a beautiful message that I can truly relate to on so many
levels. Wouldn't it be nice for our classroom community to experience nineteen
picture books intentionally selected by each of you to ensure your child sees
themselves represented within the study? I will select many books, too, but your
contributions will provide a different perspective. This study is one of the many*

ways I hope to get you involved in the curriculum. I plan to showcase the books via the blog each week. Here is how it goes:

1. *Select a book that represents some aspect of your child. This can be a character trait, ethnicity, set of values, experience, culture, and so on. (Research shows that young children are empowered to read when they see both themselves and others represented in the literature available to them.)*

2. *Send the book to school with your child by October 10th. If you are having a hard time locating the book, just email me the title. Let me know if you need to have the book returned by a particular date. As you can imagine, it will take me a while to get through nineteen wonderful selections.*

3. *Send me a brief email or note explaining your choice. I will share this portion with the students, unless you don't want me to do so. If you would prefer to come read the selection in person, just email me. (I will preview the books and notes prior to them being read either way.)*

Figure 3.5
Tiffany's Letter Home Explaining Family Book Recommendations

Over the course of a few months Tiffany reads each book and helps her young students build discussions around what they notice, what they appreciate, and what they wonder. The combination of purposeful texts and rich classroom discussion allows her students to get to know their new friends while at the same time recognizing and showing appreciation for aspects of their individual and collective identities that may otherwise be overlooked.

As is likely the case for many of us, the experiences in Tiffany's classroom are in direct contrast to her own experiences as a kindergarten student many years ago. She reflects:

> When I was the same age as the kids in my classroom, I don't remember my teacher ever trying to figure out who I was. In fact, she did just the opposite. She made assumptions based on my physical appearance and where I came from. Nothing else. She never made an effort to get to know me or my family or the things I loved. There was never an opportunity for me to show I was anything more than her assumptions. I want better for my own teaching. I want better for the kids in my classroom. We can learn so much when we're willing to stop and listen to our kids.

Creating opportunities for our kids to share themselves can be a transformative process. Such was the case in Tiffany's classroom when Maison walked in one morning excited to share his book (see Figure 3.6). Titled *Stuttering Stephen*, it told the story of a young boy who's embarrassed and frustrated by his persistent stutter. Given the opportunity to share an important piece of himself, Maison stood beside Tiffany and immediately took control. He began by questioning his classmates and providing some contextual knowledge.

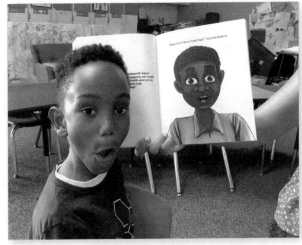

Figure 3.6
Maison Poses Next to His Family Recommendation Book

> **Maison:** I want to ask ya'll a question. How many of y'all stutter or know someone who stutters?
>
> **Classmate 1:** Maison, what is stuttering?
>
> **Maison:** Stuttering is when you have a hard time gettin' words out sometimes.

Hands raised all around the room as kids and adults alike shared times they'd struggled with their own words for a variety of reasons—nervousness, overexcitement, forgetting what they were about to say. After Tiffany read the book aloud, Maison's classmates shared responses revealing their growing ability to identify with and better understand the frustration Maison feels each day when his words just won't come out.

> **Maison:** Does anyone have any questions or comments?
>
> **Classmate 1:** Maison, I really like your book a lot. Sometimes, when I get nervous I stutter. My little cousin stutters, too.
>
> **Classmate 2:** Yeah, that was a really good book. I'm glad Stuttering Stephen didn't give up when his classmates were being mean. He should be in [our class]. We wouldn't laugh at him.

Like so many of the books his classmates shared during this inquiry, Maison's story offered an opportunity for students to see that diversity can take many forms—not only in their classroom but in the larger community as well. Yet, the kids in the classroom weren't the only ones learning from one another. As the classroom teacher, Tiffany gained powerful information throughout this literature study about her children and their families that allowed her to better develop a culturally responsive curriculum, access culturally relevant resources, and build positive social identities for each and every child in her classroom.

Watch ▶

Deep Community Building with Students and Families: In this clip, Chris interviews kindergarten teacher Tiffany Palmatier on how knowing her students informs her curriculum.

Sharing Our Cultural Knowledge: In this clip, second grader Zaina shares her knowledge of Arabic, which invites other children to share their knowledge of languages besides English.

When classrooms continue to narrowly define what counts as relevant . . . they not only turn a blind eye to the many contributions made by those from marginalized communities but also become part of a larger system of oppression that acts to normalize the dominance of those in power.

How Children Navigate Diverse Perspectives

4

From the very first day our students walk into the classroom, they're prepared to begin discussing what they feel is and is not fair. After all, they've been doing this their whole lives. Since their earliest days as a toddler they have been developing a set of personal beliefs to help them distinguish between *right* and *wrong*, *good* and *bad*. As discussed in Chapter 2, many of these beliefs have been formed through authority, a priori, and tenacity and are largely shaped by their own narrow experiences and desires.

Yet, when students enter our classrooms and engage in discussions designed to explore what is and is not just, they often find it's far more complicated to find a consensus than they expected. That's because not everyone enters these discussions with the same experiences or perspectives. For this reason, our justice-oriented discussions can become tricky to navigate. In this chapter I will demonstrate a framework (see Figure 4.1) for analyzing how students make sense of and speak back to oppression. Identifying the perspectives students take allows us to be better prepared to be successful in facilitating these discussions.

The first question is whether each participant in the discussion accepts oppressive beliefs and practices as real problems. The second level of analysis is to determine how students are making sense of the issue. And lastly, the third question examines what these beliefs allow students to either preserve (forms of injustice or oppression) or disrupt (unjust beliefs and practices). Considering each of these carefully, we can make better sense of student responses and determine how best to respond, when necessary.

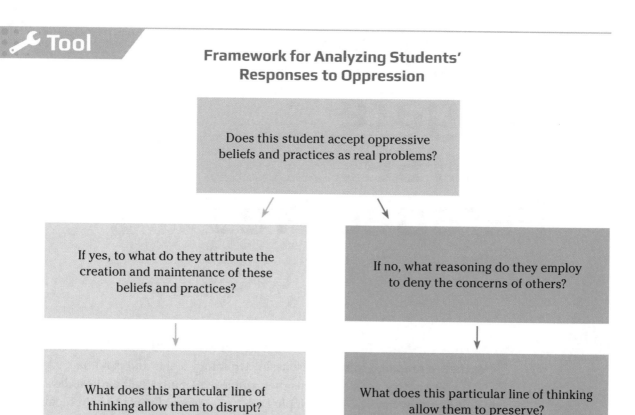

Framework for Analyzing Students' Responses to Oppression

Does this student accept oppressive beliefs and practices as real problems?

If yes, to what do they attribute the creation and maintenance of these beliefs and practices?

If no, what reasoning do they employ to deny the concerns of others?

What does this particular line of thinking allow them to disrupt?

What does this particular line of thinking allow them to preserve?

Figure 4.1

Framework for Analyzing Students' Responses to Oppression

This chapter is organized into two parts. The first section, "Students Accepting Injustice," details three frames students in my classroom often use when making sense of issues they accept as real and unjust. The second section, "Students Denying Injustice," examines the stances students often take when unable or unwilling to accept an injustice is real.

Students Accepting Injustice

When someone calls attention to an act they feel is unjust, there's often a divide between those who want to begin making sense of this phenomenon and those who feel the claim is based on a false assumption or inaccurate observation. It's often these debates over whether or not an injustice is real (say, racial profiling) that prevent our nation from moving ahead in creating meaningful solutions. The same is true in our classrooms.

When children accept injustices as real, they develop theories to explain how and why these may exist. When I analyze my students' responses, I notice many of their explanations tend to fall within one of three frames:

- the existence of a power differential between social groups

- people acting to maintain the status quo

- people forming opinions based on stereotypes.

I refer to each of these as "frames" because they define how we see the problem. Once I notice these frames emerge, I can begin naming them for the class. For instance, here we are discussing efforts made to keep Black people from voting.

> **Malik:** I think the reason they couldn't vote is because all the white people didn't want them to because they were afraid they might vote for someone else.
>
> **Chris:** What do you mean? How would the white people have stopped them from voting?
>
> **Noah:** Like, they weren't allowed to. The law said they couldn't vote.
>
> **Chris:** Ah, yeah. So the white people made laws keeping others from being able to vote. They had a whole lot of *power* to make decisions for other people because they were the ones voting and creating the laws. In terms of running the cities, states, and country, they had too much power. It wasn't being shared fairly.

As I work to make sense of what I hear them trying to say and name back to them generative frames they can use over and over, we create a shared language within our classroom. In this section I will share how our class defines these three particular frames (see Figure 4.2)—power, status quo thinking, and the role of stereotypes—as well as demonstrate how my kids implement these into their analysis of oppressive beliefs and practices.

Frames Used for Social Justice Discussions

Frame	How It's Used
Power Differentials Between Social Groups	
This frame describes the times when a person or group of people has the ability to make decisions that affect outcomes for themselves or for others.	*Example from Early Childhood Classrooms:* During a read-aloud of books that celebrate senior citizens learning to read for the very first time, such as Eve Bunting's *The Wednesday Surprise* (1989) or Amy Hest's *Mr. George Baker* (2007*)*, one might invite their kids to explore why these characters would not have learned to read when they were children. *Example from Upper Elementary Classrooms:* In discussing Jim Crow laws, one may draw upon the frame of power to point out the fact that white people controlled the ability to write, pass, and enforce laws. These laws were then used to protect their own white privilege. Thus, legislative power allowed whites to maintain control of opportunities, rights, and social standing within the community.
Acting in Ways to Maintain the Status Quo	
This frame describes instances when people believe or act in a certain way simply because it's familiar to them or benefits them personally.	*Example from an Early Childhood Classroom:* During a discussion of why action figures are not referred to as *dolls*, one might suggest it's widely accepted that girls play with dolls but not boys so we change the way we talk about these toys to match what we feel is expected by our community of friends and family. *Example from an Upper Elementary Classroom:* Within a discussion about how African American English is often described by white Americans as deficient, one might suggest whites and Blacks alike have been socialized into privileging Standard American English as "real" English without having considered the fact that African American English follows established structures and rules just as any other language.

Frames Used for Social Justice Discussions

Frame	How It's Used
The Effects of Stereotyping	
This frame describes how harmful measures are taken as a result of over-simplified generalizations assigned to entire groups of people.	*Example from an Early Childhood Classroom:* While reading a book such as Cheryl Kilodavis' *My Princess Boy* (2010) that defies gender stereotypes, one might point to the role stereotyping plays in making groups of people feel bad about themselves. *Example from an Upper Elementary Classroom:* During a discussion of a wall being constructed between the United States and Mexico to curb illegal immigration, one might frame this issue as the manifestation of stereotypes (illegal immigrants as dangerous) and the ways stereotyping informs unjust practices.

Figure 4.2

Frames Used for Social Justice Discussions

Relationships of Power

I begin the year carefully using power as a frame as often as I can in my own responses to various issue-based books and Morning Meeting discussions. For instance, when reading *The Bus Ride* (Miller 2001) during a social studies lesson, a number of my white children failed to see what was the big deal about laws forcing Black people to ride on the back of the bus.

Elena: Well, I was wondering why do the white people think it was much more better to ride at the front of the bus. I don't know why they like it up there because I like the back of the bus. It's bumpier.

Chris: So that makes me wonder, Elena, was it really about the front of the bus being better than the back of the bus or was it about people being told what they could and couldn't do?

Alan: I have a connection to Elena. At Punta Cana we rode on these buses to go to different places and I liked the back the best because it was very, very bumpy.

Chris: Right, and I think people appreciate having the power to choose for themselves—not have others choose for them—where they're allowed to sit. It's not the seat that's important here so much as the ability for people to be free to make their own choices. If the white people have the *power* to make laws that take away freedom from Black people, that is unjust. Furthermore, if Black people don't have the *power* to make laws or to even vote for the people making these laws, we have lots and lots of problems. No single group should hold all this power.

Power is an incredibly important concept for children to understand. Understanding and recognizing the role power plays allows students to begin tracing injustices back to their causes (the preservation of white privilege, the preservation of male privilege, etc.). As I continue to point out the imbalance of power between various social groups, a number of my students eventually begin to notice this as well. To illustrate, I'll share two classroom vignettes.

Socioeconomic power

During Briana's discussion about why Black people are viewed as bad when there are white people committing the very same crimes, Kumail proposed race was not the only factor at play. He suggested there were power differentials, as well, based on socioeconomics.

Chris: Hmm, so these are all good thoughts to consider. Getting back to Briana's concern, I'm wondering why the news media does focus so much of their attention on Black crime.

Kumail: Maybe it's because the news people are white and it's mostly white people who are richer. Because the richest man is a white person. So maybe that's what makes them think whites commit less crime. They think they're richer than "these small Black people" and maybe it's because those people had slaves and because they thought they were richer they were like "These people are poor. They can do work for me."

Chris: Well, there are lots of wealthy Black people as well but you are absolutely right, Kumail. As a whole, white people hold far too much of the wealth and with that comes power.

Referring back to the days of slavery as historical context for this issue, Kumail points to a long-standing power differential between the wealthy and the poor: "They think they're richer than 'these small Black people,'" he says, surmising that greater wealth has allowed whites not only to exert power over Blacks but also, because of their elevated socioeconomic status, to feel justified in doing so—such as in the case of white news anchors creating reality for viewers when reporting on Black crime.

Racial power

Discussions of race often find students using the frame of power to explain the struggles facing communities of Color. In the following vignette, someone has asked why the United States has had only one Black president. Noah, searching for just the right word to articulate his thoughts, uses the construct of power to explain how the Black community was unable, for so many years, to determine significant parts of their own outcomes beyond just becoming president.

> **Noah:** I think one of the reasons is because a long time ago Black people didn't have that much power, like in authority. I don't know what kind of word I'm looking for—but now Black people have more power and are able to do more things than back then. Back then they were, like, disabled through laws.

In evoking power as a frame for his explanation, Noah stated Black people "were, like, disabled through laws" to implicate the white community as complicit in these injustices. Doing so positioned his classmates to consider the fact that the difficulty was not just Blacks working to gain power but whites working to keep it from them. Once the frame of power was established ("Black people didn't have that much power, like in authority"), Noah named a specific way unjust forces were at work to cripple the Black community—disabling them through laws.

Analysis

When students accept an injustice as real and then suggest power is a key factor in helping us understand how this injustice has been maintained over time, they bring us to our third level of analysis (Figure 4.3).

By choosing to accept these issues as problematic and then identifying relationships of power as a driving force in their maintenance, Kumail and Noah have taken the first step in disrupting these oppressive practices. The hypotheses they offer reveal power imbalances at play as well as offer the potential for action.

This level of analysis allows us to outgrow the desire to sum up inquiries into justice by simply saying "This is just awful because everyone should be equal" and

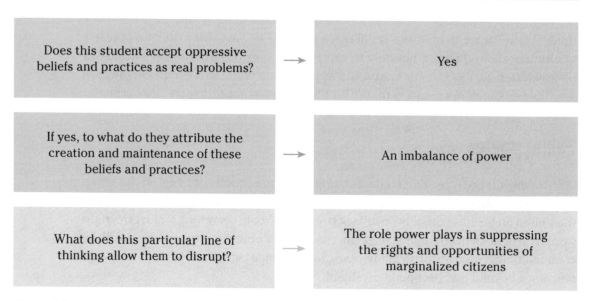

| Does this student accept oppressive beliefs and practices as real problems? | → | Yes |

| If yes, to what do they attribute the creation and maintenance of these beliefs and practices? | → | An imbalance of power |

| What does this particular line of thinking allow them to disrupt? | → | The role power plays in suppressing the rights and opportunities of marginalized citizens |

Figure 4.3

Third Level of Analysis: Disruption of Power to Suppress

instead push our kids to begin taking action. Three questions can lead us down this path:

- Who holds the power?
- What allows them to maintain this power?
- What can be done to disrupt this?

If we're to position our kids as primary meaning makers (a worthwhile goal), we should be careful to avoid having the final say in each and every discussion. Questions such as those posed above offer us a great path to achieving this. That said, our students need some scaffolding to get there. We'll need to be prepared to spend quite some time thinking aloud in front of them in addition to providing as much historical context as possible in the form of children's books and current news articles. With time and patience, our students learn not only to dissect injustices but even to decide what actions can be taken to disrupt these—either in their personal lives (critiquing their own prejudiced thinking) or in efforts to transform the beliefs and practices of others in the community.

Maintenance of the Status Quo

Students also often demonstrate a belief that each new generation, knowingly or unknowingly, accepts and acts upon the established beliefs and practices of past generations. Over time we come to refer to this blind acceptance of what has always been as "status quo thinking." In the following example, Kumail responds during a discussion of how various cultures have come to think of males as more capable leaders than females. To create a historical context, Kumail imagined what the first days of humans must have been like.

> **Kumail:** Like when humans first came on this planet, there was usually boys who risked their lives to hunt down big creatures and the women took care of all the kids. And maybe because from that time, when only men had those weapons, they were the hunters and they had to do that work. From that time . . . on this part of the earth everyone kept thinking that since girls started out like that that's how they stayed until this time, taking care of the house and the kids while the men went out to do other things.

Kumail's love of nonfiction reading provided him a developing understanding of what prehistoric times were like. In accessing this information he suggests a connection between the beliefs and practices of the past and those of the present. In a later discussion about the lack of female presidents, Imani also argued that people tend to fall into previously established patterns when making sense of the world and their expectations for the people in it. Here, she hypothesizes about why there has yet to be a woman in the Oval Office.

> **Imani:** I think it's because the first president George Washington, he was well, you know, a boy. And the next president was a boy. And the next president was a boy. So everyone just got used to the girls living in the White House and the boys being president.

As Imani suggested an origin of how women have come to be underrepresented throughout the history of our country, she called attention to the relationship between a person's gender and their political opportunities during the eighteenth century. As Kumail and Imani tracked these oppressive beliefs and practices all the way back to early humans and the creation of our government, neither suggested an active effort on the part of a dominant group to exert power but, rather, suggested these beliefs and practices were mindlessly carried out as people operated within their understanding of how the world already worked. We know, of course, this is not entirely true at all. There have been and continue to be a number of deliberate efforts to curtail the rights and opportunities of many social groups. That said, it's important students understand that people can mindlessly adopt and carry out social norms without ever questioning whether or not they are accurate or just.

Analysis

Identifying the ways people act to maintain the status quo allows students to see there are times when people act in oppressive ways or accept the presence of unjust practices without being fully aware they're even doing so. For instance, there was a time in my life when the idea of a female pastor was very foreign to me. It wasn't that I didn't think women were capable of holding this post, but I'd become so accustomed to seeing men at the head of the church that I never stopped to question why this was and what it meant for women. For much of my childhood I just mindlessly accepted this as a "job for men." It wasn't until later in life, when something I said along these same lines was directly challenged by someone, that I began to reconsider the validity of my belief as well as the effect it had, when held by millions of others, on women. Once our students begin to identify examples of people working to blindly maintain the status quo, we can help them identify the need for greater reflection and critique. This leads us to our third level of analysis. See Figure 4.4.

As with an understanding of the role power plays in oppressing groups of people, when students begin to acknowledge ways people work to maintain the status quo, they take the first steps toward disrupting injustice. Our next step in supporting them is to pose carefully crafted questions.

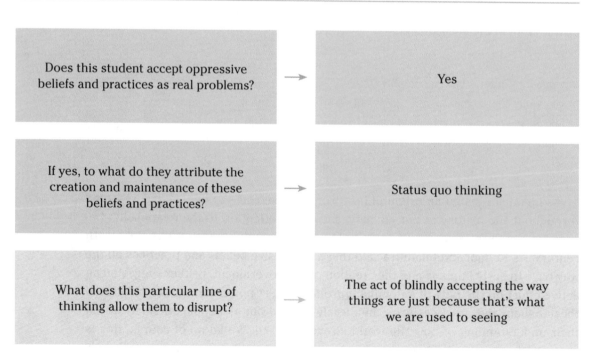

Figure 4.4

Third Level of Analysis: Disruption of Blind Acceptance

If people simply do this because it's what they're used to . . .

- Who does it benefit?
- Do we play an active (or passive) role in this?
- What can we do to disrupt it?

Listen in as Imani's statements are fleshed out more fully using similar questions.

Imani: I think it's because the first president George Washington, he was well, you know, a boy. And the next president was a boy. And the next president was a boy. So everyone just got used to the girls living in the White House and the boys being president.

Chris: Hmm. That's possible. I would say, though, there have been many times when men have acted to make sure women had very limited power—like refusing them voting rights, educational opportunities, and so on. But you're right, people sometimes do things just because it's what they're used to doing and seeing others do. In this case, if people expected only men to be the ones who were in charge of the country and the states and the cities by holding office, who did this benefit?

Peter: It benefited the men.

Chris: Right, but why?

Elena: Because they got to be the ones in charge. And I don't think it's right that the men did that.

Chris: But you know one thing that's interesting is there were some cases when the women agreed the men should be in charge. In fact, there were many cases of this.

Elena: What?

Chris: Well, because a number of them were so used to seeing men take those offices and go to college to become lawyers and doctors and things like that, some women stopped questioning whether this was wrong. They just got really used to it. Not all women. Not at all. Lots knew it was wrong and fought against it. But for some they believed this was OK. That's what can happen when we get so used to something and we stop asking questions and wondering whether or not it's fair.

Malia: I wouldn't have done that. I'd be mad.

Chris: But I wonder if there's any times in our own lives when we do the same thing? Thinking of women being in charge, do we ever do anything that helps people keep believing men are better or smarter or stronger? Do we sometimes play a role?

[*Long silence*]

Laila: Well, I think maybe like earlier in the year when people talked about how sometimes people laugh when a girl beats a boy at something.

Chris: What do you mean?

Laila: Like, if people laugh because a girl wins, they're saying boys are better and shouldn't lose.

Alan: I don't laugh when boys lose.

Elena: But some boys do.

Colton: Yeah, well some girls do, too. I've seen them.

Chris: Aah, that's exactly what I was thinking about. It seems like there are times when many of us—maybe even all of us—need to be more careful about the messages we send. Maybe these messages help others hold on to those harmful beliefs. Any ideas on what we could do to disrupt this? What could we do to change the way we and others think and act?

Alan: People could stop laughing when the girls beat the boys.

Chris: OK. What else?

As with our questions related to the maintenance of power, engaging kids in this line of thinking positions them as the primary meaning makers and calls on them to generate solutions that will lead to a more just classroom and a more just society.

Effect of Learned Stereotypes

One other way students often frame an issue is to call attention to the role stereotyping plays in mistreating and undervaluing others. For instance, in the following discussion about why it seems so many cultures have been slow to recognize the academic and leadership potential of females, Martin and Peter suggest this might be related to how females are sometimes viewed by males.

Martin: Um, maybe they just don't think girls can do what boys can do. Like, they think it's a new thing for them and they don't think girls can do that.

Chris: Yeah, obviously they don't think girls can do it and it seems their opinions hold a lot of power. Why do you think they don't believe women or girls can or should be leaders? Where does that come from?

Martin speaks to the role of lowered expectations and, identifying the power males often hold in these situations to make influential decisions, implies that power and stereotypes work hand in hand to deny equal access to leadership roles. Later in the same discussion, Peter echoes Martin's thought when naming specific beliefs some males have about the potential of women.

> **Peter:** Well, probably people think that boys are stronger than girls and they think that men can do more stuff than girls can. And they probably think that girls shouldn't be president because all those men who have been president.
>
> **Chris:** OK, so that whole idea of men being stronger or more powerful or being better prepared to be a leader. I think it would be interesting for us to think about where we get those messages. Where are we learning about these stereotypes? Are we seeing it on TV? Are we seeing it in books? Are people telling us this? I don't remember my parents ever telling me things like that but I remember those sorts of ideas being there.

It's interesting to note that although both Martin and Peter speak to the negative consequences gender stereotypes can have on females, each uses the pronoun *they* when naming who was passing on these hurtful and harmful notions. This shifting of the blame is a common practice even when the very same unchecked beliefs reside within our own minds and hearts. Kids do it. We do it, too. By distancing ourselves from these acts, we allow ourselves to continue feeling safe within critical discussions because we operate as though we're not part of the problem. But what does this get us? Our kids' desire, *our* desire, to be seen as one of the "good ones" cannot and should not relieve any of us of our responsibility to be truly reflective and, when necessary, to change.

Analysis

Critiquing the effects of stereotyping should be a key aspect of classroom discussions. As history has shown time and again, one of the most effective ways of maintaining power and privilege is to lead people to falsely believe hierarchies are a natural outcome where those who are most capable and deserving earn what is rightfully theirs. The maintenance of stereotypes depicting women as weak, people of Color as lazy, or the LGBTQIA+ community as mentally ill works in strategic ways not only to smear these groups but to legitimize the unearned and unwarranted privileges of so many others. When our students begin to identify the role stereotypes play in the maintenance of various injustices, we can then consider our third level of analysis: How does this knowledge prepare us to take action? See Figure 4.5.

When students begin to acknowledge the role stereotypes play in maintaining power for some while denying it to others, they take the first steps toward

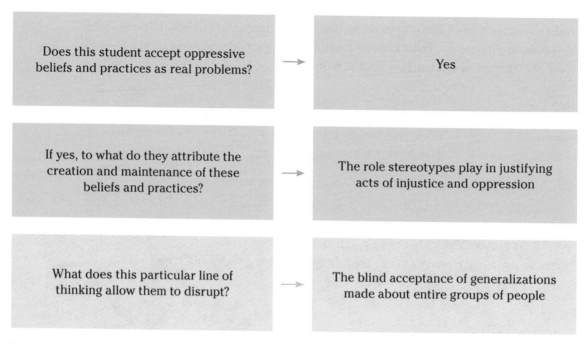

Figure 4.5

Third Level of Analysis: Disruption of Overgeneralization

disrupting these injustices. Our next step in supporting them is to pose carefully crafted questions.

- Who do these stereotypes benefit?
- How do these stereotypes help dominant social groups maintain their power?
- What can we do to disrupt the spread of such stereotypes?

As with both power and maintenance of the status quo, we can use carefully selected questions to help our students dissect the nature of injustice and then develop plans of action to push back against these injustices. In this way, we take on not only opportunities in our classrooms to teach our kids to love and embrace diversity but also act as allies dedicated to abolishing systemic injustice and oppression.

Students Denying Injustice

Not all students are quite so willing to take this journey of thought with us. They listen to the questions being posed by their teacher and classmates, they hear the personal thoughts and experiences shared by others, yet they fail to see the problematic nature of any of this. Although this refusal to acknowledge inequities can emerge from many places, I've noticed two perspectives in particular that tend to show up quite often in our class discussions. One is the belief that the world is an inherently fair place and that any experiences challenging this can simply be explained away. The other belief is that such claims are either exaggerations or outright lies where people are being overly sensitive to things that aren't really that big of a deal.

The World Is a Fair Place

A very common perspective of those who fail to recognize the significance of systemic injustices and oppressions is the belief that there must be a logical explanation for these so-called injustices. In these instances, students resist the suggestion of wrongdoing in an effort to maintain their desire to see the world as a fair place to all. At times, these students even place blame back at the feet of those being oppressed. For instance, when Briana asked why there was a lack of Black characters on her favorite television shows, Martin was quick to suggest it may be the Black community's fault for not trying to get these roles.

Martin: I think they just couldn't find enough Black people to play on the shows.

Chris: There weren't enough actors and actresses who were Black?

Martin: Yeah, like they couldn't find them. Whenever they were looking for people to play in the show they just couldn't find enough Black people.

Alan: Yeah, they just couldn't.

By stating there weren't enough Black actors and actresses showing up for casting calls, Martin shifts the blame from television networks and casting directors to those Black actors who *do* show up only to be denied these roles. As is often the case in these instances, Martin believed America provides a level playing field for all, and when confronted with information challenging this, he created an explanation that allowed him to retain his worldview. In my experience, this tendency to create excuses to explain away any suggestions of injustice is especially typical among white students. Because they don't feel the weight of these inequities and have nothing to lose, they fail to recognize them as problematic.

In another discussion about representation, this time looking at the lack of children's books about people of Color (see Figure 4.6), two other students worked hard to retain the belief the world is a fair place for all. In this vignette, I had just shared a data set from the University of Wisconsin showing roughly 1,558 of the 2,270 children's books about human characters the University received the previous year were directly about or reflected white characters and white culture and significantly

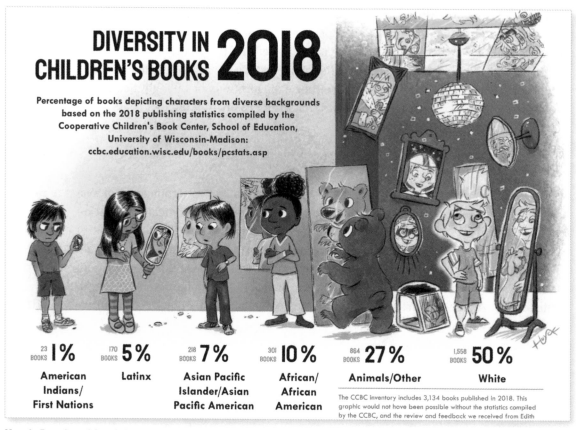

DIVERSITY IN CHILDREN'S BOOKS 2018

Percentage of books depicting characters from diverse backgrounds based on the 2018 publishing statistics compiled by the Cooperative Children's Book Center, School of Education, University of Wisconsin-Madison: ccbc.education.wisc.edu/books/pcstats.asp

23 BOOKS **1%** American Indians/ First Nations

170 BOOKS **5%** Latinx

218 BOOKS **7%** Asian Pacific Islander/Asian Pacific American

301 BOOKS **10%** African/ African American

864 BOOKS **27%** Animals/Other

1,558 BOOKS **50%** White

The CCBC inventory includes 3,134 books published in 2018. This graphic would not have been possible without the statistics compiled by the CCBC, and the review and feedback we received from Edith

Huyck, David, and Sarah Park Dahlen. (2019 June 19). Diversity in Children's Books 2018. *sarahpark.com* blog. Created in consultation with Edith Campbell, Molly Beth Griffin, K. T. Horning, Debbie Reese, Ebony Elizabeth Thomas, and Madeline Tyner, with statistics compiled by the Cooperative Children's Book Center, School of Education, University of Wisconsin-Madison: http://ccbc.education.wisc.edu/books/pcstats.asp. Retrieved from https://readingspark.word press.com/2019/06/19/picture-this-diversity-in-childrens-books-2018-infographic/.

Figure 4.6

Representation in Children's Literature

fewer books reflected other groups such as Blacks, Latinx, Native Americans, and Asian Americans.

> Chris: All right, who wants to share out? Why do you think there's such a big difference? Because it *is* a big difference. It's not like it's 400 to 300. It's 1,558 to 301. And it's 1,558 to 170. And it's 1,558 to 23. Why do you think there's such a big difference between the number of books about white people and culture and other groups of people who live here?

Gabby: I think it's because more white people live here than Black people, and I think that this country is more like where white people live. Normally Black people live across the ocean. And so a lot of different people than white aren't here and so they write more books about white people.

Gabby begins by claiming the overwhelming dominance of white characters in this data set is due to the fact "normally Black people live across the ocean"—a statement meant to support her understanding of America as primarily white. Using population size to defend the lack of representation or all-out exclusion of minoritized groups across various fields and media sources is a common argument made by students who fit within dominant social groups such as white, middle-class, and Christian. Although two Black students in the class claimed this was "unfair" and "disrespectful," many of the white students felt such practices within the publishing world were logical outcomes and not at all unjust.

Other rationalizations are often offered as well. In the following excerpt the class is discussing the treatment of Blacks during the 1950s and 1960s. Kumail implies whites may have had a justifiable claim to their power.

Emily: I was thinking about when you said that Black people had to have their own water fountain, their own stores, and—

Braden: Their own stores?

Emily: Their own *school* . . . I was thinking about that and I was wondering, I was thinking people care more about white people than they do about Black people because they're—I think because like white people could talk to Black people but Black people couldn't talk to white people. I thought that was pretty selfish—

Alan: I know!

Emily: —and usually there was a lot of stores for white people to go to but there was like barely any for Black people.

Kumail: It's because the white people came to America before the Black people. That's why.

Similar to the practice of using population sizes to legitimize white dominance, Kumail, an Indian American, references the fact that whites came to America before Blacks to suggest whites were entitled to a higher status. Accessing a common argument students use in their own lives, "I was here first!," Kumail offers justification for the racist actions of whites rather than an indictment of their motives, beliefs, or practices. In each of these cases, non-Black students failed to empathize or see these issues from the perspective of those being oppressed—as discriminatory actions designed to further establish and preserve white privilege.

It's Exaggerated or Untrue

Another common perspective taken by students from culturally dominant groups is to assume the significance of injustice issues is being overstated or exaggerated. For instance, when speaking to an article detailing that girls shopping for Halloween costumes at a poplar outlet had only three career-oriented costume choices as opposed to seventeen such selections for boys, Martin failed to see the problem, stating:

> **Martin:** I think the girl in the article should just choose one of the three costumes at the store and then hope she gets lucky next year. Maybe they'll have more.

In electing not to address any wrong on the part of the store, Martin implied this was largely a nonissue and that girls would do best to accept what is and hope for better outcomes in the future. Later, he went even further in suggesting too much was being made of this.

> **Martin:** Well, it could be worse. The girls could've had no costume choices at all.

Martin's perspective regarding the inequality of Halloween costume choices demonstrates how members of the culturally dominant group are often dismissive of claims that pose no direct threat to their own lives. Although many of the girls were in agreement the store should simply combine all costumes and market them to both boys and girls, Martin held fast to his belief this wasn't necessary because it just wasn't that big of a deal.

There are times, too, when students from culturally dominant groups do more than simply belittle the injustices experienced by others, but work to deny their very existence. For example, in response to Briana's question about why Black people are viewed differently than white people, Elena and Peter were quick to disagree.

> **Briana:** Why do people say mostly all Black people are bad and not that much white people?
>
> **Elena:** No one thinks that.
>
> **Peter:** Yeah, no one thinks that.

Neither believed there was a need to entertain Briana's question, given the fact their perspectives as white children had shielded them from recognizing the ways *Black as bad* is implicitly communicated in so many ways, including the reporting of crime. Briana's perspective as a Black child allowed her to acknowledge this because it directly affected her. She saw it everywhere and, as evidenced during her time in our classroom, was not shy about bringing it to her classmates' attention. Yet, she often struggled to help many of them accept this as truth.

Time and again I notice children from culturally dominant groups struggle to accept the experiences and concerns of those from marginalized social groups because what they are hearing does not reflect their own experiences. A powerfully illustrative example of this occurred during a discussion one morning where I shared the acts of racism my Black son had experienced during his time in middle school. I told this story to help illustrate the fact there are many harmful perspectives to be found in our community and that we need to play an active role in disrupting them. Hearing this, Kumail became frustrated because, given his own experiences, he felt we were exaggerating these stories.

Kumail: When I first came to this school people would call my food *poop*. But then other people—Black people in this class—they never said anything bad about them. But they did about me. But I'm from a different country. They're Black people.

Chris: Right.

Kumail: And you're saying some people say that it's Black people getting treated badly. I don't think that's true. In this class no Black person is treated badly but I was once treated badly.

Alan: It's like when Kumail first came we . . . *some* people thought he couldn't do things the way we could.

Imani: Yeah, when we first came to kindergarten people thought his food was weird.

Kumail understood and accepted past stories of slavery and segregation as racist but had not noticed any evidence of present-day racism within our school or in his larger community. Introducing his own experiences as an Indian American, he used his story to challenge whether or not the Black community truly is mistreated. I loved the courage of his statement; although it was misinformed as to the lived experiences of Black Americans, it did bring to light the tendency of our discussions to frame race and race-related issues as a dichotomy of whiteness and Blackness rather than working hard enough to include the experiences of others, such as Indian Americans. Up to that point, many class discussions addressing Kumail's frustrations with others had focused on his religious beliefs as a Hindu and the unwillingness of some Christians in class to accept and respect his beliefs. However, Kumail's opposition to our discussions of current-day racism revealed that it was more than his religious identity that positioned him as different. In doing so, Kumail rightly pushed for broader discussions of race.

These examples—Martin's softening of sexist costume choices, Elena and Peter's refusal to accept Briana's observation of the ways society views Black people, and Kumail's claim we were addressing the wrong issues—illustrate yet again the role identity plays in our ability to make sense of social justice. Without intentional efforts to help our students see the world through the eyes of others, the problems facing our society will only continue.

Analysis

No matter what logic or motivation students use to explain away the existence of inequities, the outcome is always the same: a preservation of unearned privileges and cultural dominance. See Figure 4.7.

So what do we do when our students do not see the problematic nature of denying service to a Muslim ("They could just make their own stores and not let other people

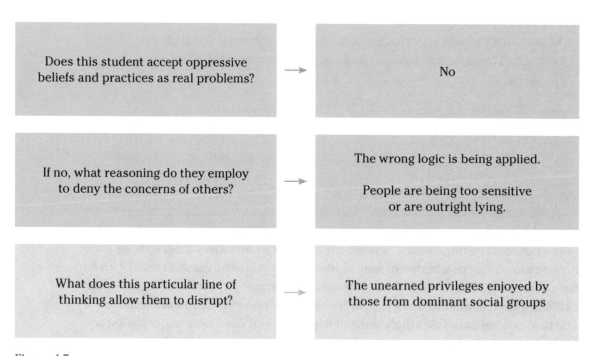

Figure 4.7
Third Level of Analysis: Preservation of Unearned Privilege

in"), full rights to gay couples ("They could just live together and not get married"), or humane treatment of those seeking asylum ("I'd just stay in my own country and hope it gets better"). We essentially have five options we can employ individually or in combination with one another.

1. Tell the student they're wrong.

2. Coerce the student to agree with us.

3. Avoid responding to their statement altogether and move on.

4. Tell the student it's OK to have differing perspectives.

5. Invite the class to keep thinking about this.

Before quickly settling on any one of these as the "best" option, we should first consider the nature of what's been said. For instance, if a student has challenged whether or not stereotypes are harmful and, in fact, has declared certain stereotypes are actually true, we have a moral responsibility to speak back to this in a very direct manner. Our task in these situations is to challenge what has been said, reveal how such beliefs work to oppress entire groups of people, and offer contrasting information to reveal a more accurate take on reality. In essence, we ensure the class knows such statements are wrong.

However, most responses are not likely to take the form of a direct attack on any person or group of people. The maintenance of systemic injustice is largely built upon the overwhelming presence of a softer brand of dominance. This is the type that claims to want the best for all people yet consistently falls short of truly hearing all voices or considering all concerns. These are words spoken by those who can't step outside their own lived experiences to consider what it might be like to walk in someone else's shoes. On a national stage we see this time and again as straight people try to tell the gay community how they can be "fixed," white people try to tell the Black community how they can find greater success and acceptance, and men try to tell women how to feel about "innocent" gestures or sexual advances. Dominant social groups love to claim they want nothing more than to help, yet they often expect those within marginalized social groups to change themselves first to meet the needs of the dominant culture. If members of the LGBTQIA+ community have to hide pieces of their identity to be accepted by straights, the Black community has to code switch to have their academic brilliance recognized by whites, or women have to endure situations that make them feel uncomfortable or unsafe to maintain a happy work environment for men, these dominant groups are not working to hear the voices, concerns, or needs of those for whom they claim to care.

This is what's at risk when cultural dominance is supported in our classroom through perspectives that continually question the legitimacy of injustice and oppression. As classroom teachers we are on the front lines of this battle for equality. How we choose to respond is critical.

Watch ▶

Expectations for Our Children Over Time:
Teacher and parent Susanne discusses how
she's seen her son come in and out of social
justice awareness.

Challenges in Homogenous Classrooms:
Teacher Nozsa Tinsley discusses how the
work can differ in school settings.

Our kids' desire, *our* desire, to be seen as one of the "good ones" cannot and should not relieve any of us of our responsibility to be truly reflective and, when necessary, to change.

Using Issue-Based Literature

5

How do we support students in understanding what it truly means to be just? In this chapter, we'll explore how to include social justice texts in our reading and social studies curricula. When we use such texts, we frame our instruction within a larger purpose with only small changes to our planning. Our goals will be to help students (1) build cultural competency as they come to better understand and empathize with the experiences of others and (2) gain the historical knowledge they need to contextualize issues of today.

Goal 1: Using Issue-Based Texts to Build Understanding and Empathy

In Chapter 3 we shared the importance of texts that reflect the many particulars of students' lives and identities. Making deliberate book choices not only affirms our students' identities but also helps them build positive social identities. That is essential but not enough. Literature provides a unique opportunity for children to expand the circle of people they know who have been impacted by injustice. Through fictional characters and historical figures, children can better empathize with others' lived experiences. You'll see in this chapter that it's not hard to deliberately incorporate such texts in your regular conventional curriculum.

As much as we'd like to believe empathy and respect for marginalized groups of people is on the rise, recent studies have shown this may be wishful thinking. As part of ongoing research into youth and racism in America, sociologist Margaret Hagerman (2018) found an alarming number of white children tend to demonstrate racial apathy in response to acts of racism. In her study, this apathy took two forms. The first was to *dismiss the significance of racism*. For example, when asked if they believed Donald Trump had said racist things during his 2016 campaign and ensuing presidency, a number of white children admitted to having heard the President say racist things but ultimately felt it wasn't that big of a deal ("I honestly think it's fine. It doesn't bother me."). The second form of apathy was to *outright deny the existence of racism* in Trump's beliefs or anywhere within their communities. One young girl, Ellie, said she hadn't heard Trump say anything racist and did not see racism as an issue in her community. She explained, "There's not really any [racism] going on in Mississippi, but there might be in like, other states, I just haven't noticed anything . . . I don't really know . . . It's not something I care about." As part of the privileged race, racism isn't something Ellie is forced to address or even acknowledge as the system in place already works to her benefit.

Likely, this is not a topic Ellie has explored with people of Color. If she's discussed it at all, it's probably been at home or with close friends who share the same unearned racial privileges she does. Such small circles of influence provide a homogenous bubble with few opportunities to see the world through any other perspective but her own. Given the fact so many students from the dominant culture live within that same homogenous bubble, we shouldn't be surprised by their inability (or at times, unwillingness) to recognize systemic injustices—not to mention recognizing their own complicit role in maintaining them. Like so many of us, these students need to build greater cultural competency. Fortunately, schools are powerful sites for this work. In most places classrooms offer an opportunity to work in community with a wide diversity of peers. And even in schools that appear from the outside to be quite homogenous, classrooms offer an opportunity to engage with diverse literature and perspectives that push students to interact with others in hopes of better understanding, appreciating, and empathizing with the complex lives and concerns of others.

As I write this, my class and I are in the midst of such work. I recently came across a book that is new to me, Queen Rania Al Abdullah and Kelly DiPucchio's *The Sandwich Swap* (2010). This short tale tells the story of two friends who find themselves temporarily at odds over ugly statements each has made about the contents of the other's lunch. Salma feels hurt by insults launched at her hummus sandwich, and Lilly feels equally hurt by remarks directed at her peanut butter sandwich. After reading this book as part of an inquiry into author's purpose, Zeina, who often brings Middle Eastern foods in her lunchbox and quickly identified with Salma's character, was eager to share. See Figure 5.1 for the details of our discussion and the moves I make to ensure these discussions are justice-oriented in content and methodology.

In the example provided, no one was specifically called out. No one was made to feel shameful. However, everyone was called on to empathize with Zeina for being made to feel different just because her foods weren't understood by others. Ezra

Key Components of Justice-Oriented Discussions

Zeina: That's like my lunch. People make fun of my food sometimes, too. ← | Follow Our Students' Lead |

Chris: What do you mean? What do they say?

Zeina: They say "That's gross" or "What is *that*?"

Abby: Yeah, I hear them say that.

Chris: Oh. So we can all probably connect to this story, can't we? Why do you think people say things like that? ← | Invite Student Analysis |

Andrew: Probably they don't know what it is. They think it's yucky.

Chris: Yeah, for some reason we sometimes feel like we need to judge things we don't understand or that are different from the things we like. ← | Acknowledge Our Role |

Zeina: It makes me sad because they say my lunch looks like bird poop.

Pierce: That's mean.

Chris: Yeah, I can imagine it would make you sad. We all could probably be a little more careful about how we respond to things we aren't familiar with. I'm curious, if this happens again, what could Zeina do? And what responsibilities do we have as bystanders watching it happen?

Following Our Students' Lead: Student-generated topics can come in multiple forms. Here, Zeina launches a discussion in response to a book we're reading together. Her connection to the story isn't brushed aside with a quick "Yeah, good point" so we can return to the content on our lesson plan. Rather, Zeina's connection becomes an opportunity to briefly explore why we sometimes fall into the trap of judging others.

Inviting Student Analysis: It can be incredibly tempting to get on our soapbox and name life lessons for our children. In this instance, I'm sure I was tempted to say, "Let me make this clear: We should never tease others for having foods different from our own. It's mean." In doing so, I could have exercised my authority over my kids to quickly establish classroom expectations. To be honest, there are times when I do this. However, more often I choose the generative approach, which is to call on them to consider what would cause people to act in a certain way. Asking questions such as "Why do you think people would act this way?" positions them to begin analyzing social beliefs in hopes of better understanding and addressing oppressive behaviors.

Recognizing Our Role: Here I shift from speaking vaguely about people who say unkind things to using the pronoun *we*. This shift places each of us at the center of the problem. My hope is to help my kids feel increasingly comfortable accepting and acknowledging their own role in these problems.

Figure 5.1

Key Components of Justice-Oriented Discussions

Hyland (2016) speaks beautifully to the potential of coming to better understand the experiences of others when declaring, "It's not until we know the stories of each other that we embrace our humanity." To embrace our humanity, we must be deliberate in drawing upon the wide variety of issues currently being taken up in children's literature—all of which are worth exploring alongside our kids. Figure 5.2 provides a small but compelling sample of some of the possibilities available to us.

 **Tool**

Issues That Can Be Explored Through Children's Literature

Issue	Titles
Gendered Norms	*My Princess Boy* by C. Kilodavis *For the Right to Learn* by R. Langston-George and J. Bock *The Paper Bag Princess* by R. Munsch
Limited Income	*Those Shoes* by M. Boelts *A Bike Like Sergio's* by M. Boelts *!Si, Se Puede! Yes, We Can! Janitor Strike in LA* by D. Cohn
Disabilities/ Differently Abled	*Emmanuel's Dream* by L. A. Thompson *We're All Wonders* by R. J. Palacio *Ian's Walk* by L. Lears
Celebrating Difference	*Stand Tall, Molly Lou Melon* by P. Lovell *Mixed* by A. Chung *I Like Myself!* by K. Beaumont
Exclusion of Others	*Each Kindness* by J. Woodson *The Invisible Boy* by T. Ludwig *The Day You Begin* by J. Woodson
Speaking Up/ Taking Action	*I Dissent* by D. Levy *Separate Is Never Equal* by D. Tonatiuh *The Youngest Marcher* by C. Levinson
Segregation	*The Bus Ride* by W. Miller *Grandmama's Pride* by B. Birtha *White Socks Only* by E. Coleman

Issues That Can Be Explored Through Children's Literature

Issue	Titles
Diverse Families and Family Structures	*The Case for Loving: The Fight for Interracial Marriage* by S. Alko *St. Elena Brings the Family* by M. B. Schiffer *Families, Families, Families!* by S. Lang
Late to Literacy	*Thank You, Mr. Falker* by P. Polacco *The Wednesday Surprise* by E. Bunting *Mr. George Baker* by A. Hest
Importance of Our Names	*The Name Jar* by Y. Choi *Chrysanthemum* by K. Henkes *Alma and How She Got Her Name* by J. Martinez-Neal
Skin Color	*Sulwe* by L. Nyong'o *All the Colors of the Earth* by S. Hamanaka *The Colors of Us* by K. Katz
Individuality	*The Day You Begin* by J. Woodson *I Am Enough* by G. Byers *Old Henry* by J. W. Blos
Differences in Hair	*Long Hair, Don't Care* by J. Guerra *Don't Touch My Hair!* by S. Miller *I Love My Hair!* by N. Anastasia Tarpley

Figure 5.2

Issues That Can Be Explored Through Children's Literature

How to Include Empathy and Understanding in Our Reading Curriculum

When we access quality books to help our students build greater understanding and empathy, we needn't worry about what we'll have to take out of the curriculum to make room. Rather, this work fits neatly within our current studies, allowing us to achieve both at the same time. We can take nearly any literacy-based curricular standard and find a way to integrate our social justice goals into the resources and practices we employ in teaching it (see Figure 5.3).

To demonstrate how this work looks in action, I'll share an example from an inquiry into reading comprehension strategies. Although I primarily draw on my professional knowledge of literacy and literacy learning when planning such an inquiry, I

 Tool

Correlation Between Reading Standards and Social Justice Work

Curriculum Standard(s)	What Are Kids Being Asked to Do?	Correlating Social Justice Goal(s)	Correlating Social Justice Skills and Strategies
Inquiry Ask self-generated questions that lead to group conversations, explorations, and investigations.	• Demonstrate curiosity/ask questions. • Build discussions/work collaboratively to construct new meanings.	• Possess a critical curiosity about the world. • Construct a strong community within the classroom. • Live alongside others in a democratic way. • Understand the value of multiple perspectives.	• Observe the world closely and ask questions about those things that seem to lack explanation. • Show genuine interest in the lives and thoughts of others. • Engage in respectful, but contested, discussion around a wide variety of topics and issues. • Seek out competing understandings and weigh these against the known facts.
Meaning and Context Compare and contrast characters' actions, feelings, and responses to major events or challenges.	• Consider the identities and experiences of various characters and how these inform their actions, feelings, and perspectives.	• Understand diversity takes on many forms and holds great value. • Understand the value of multiple perspectives.	• Understand our identities are not singular but the intersection of many social groups to which we belong. • Work to understand where competing understandings come from/the beliefs on which they are constructed.

Correlation Between Reading
Standards and Social Justice Work

Curriculum Standard(s)	What Are Kids Being Asked to Do?	Correlating Social Justice Goal(s)	Correlating Social Justice Skills and Strategies
Describe how cultural context influences characters, setting, and the development of the plot.	• Consider/examine cultural context.	• Understand diversity takes on many forms and holds great value. • Identify acts of oppression and the false beliefs that encourage people to support these acts. • Understand the value of multiple perspectives.	• Develop a deeper understanding of other cultures that moves beyond superficial understandings and challenges stereotypes. • Name the beliefs being employed to make those in power feel just in their actions. • Work to understand where competing understandings come from and the beliefs on which they are constructed.

Figure 5.3

Correlation Between Reading Standards and Social Justice Work

also access my state standards to see what specific skills and strategies will need to supplement my plans. For this study they read:

> **Standard:** Determine meaning and develop logical interpretations by making predictions, inferring, drawing conclusions, analyzing, synthesizing, providing evidence, and investigating multiple interpretations.

> **Indicator 1:** Ask and answer literal and inferential questions to demonstrate understanding of a text; use specific details to make inferences and draw conclusions in texts heard or read.

There are many ways to go about teaching comprehension. One is to introduce each of these strategies (predicting, questioning, inferring, etc.) to students and construct some sort of engagement around each that scaffolds the strategies into independent practice. If you think back to the ways we come to form new beliefs, this approach relies on students to create new knowledge through authority (hearing it is true from a trusted source). There are certainly times when this method seems most efficient. However, because I teach from an inquiry stance, I usually approach curriculum a bit differently. Whenever possible, I position students to gain new knowledge by first posing questions and then conducting research and analyzing their developing understandings alongside one another. For this particular study, I begin with the question:

> I've often said this year that "reading is thinking." If reading is thinking, what *specific* types of thinking are we doing to help us understand a text?

This is generally met with heavy doses of silence and bewilderment as the kids aren't sure where to even begin. So, we engage in the process of conducting research. Over the course of a week, I read a variety of engaging books to my kids, have them "stop and jot" their thinking onto sticky notes, and then at the end of the week ask them to work together to sort these sticky notes into different piles based on a single shared trait that can be named (for instance, a pile where they are "guessing what will happen next," "making a connection," or "asking a question"). We then spend the next few weeks diving deeper into each of the comprehension strategies they've uncovered. With this approach, I'm not telling my kids how to read for comprehension but instead helping them explicitly notice and name (Johnston 2004) the strategies they already employ so they can be more deliberate with this work in the future, thus building on what they already know how to do. Inevitably, this collaborative research leads us to the discovery that when reading we do all sorts of thinking, such as making predictions, retelling parts of the story, drawing connections, asking questions, sharing our feelings, assessing characters, and so on (see Figure 5.4).

To implement social justice goals into such an inquiry, I ask myself:

> How can this process of learning about [comprehension strategies] support the specific goals and skills I've identified as important to justice-oriented learning?

Because each study presents unique opportunities to integrate various aspects of our social justice work, our social justice goals move fluidly in and out of the curriculum at various points during the school year. For our inquiry into comprehension strategies, I knew the act of questioning the text would lend itself naturally to helping students develop a critical curiosity about the world. Specifically, I was thinking about the related skills/strategies:

- Observe the world closely and ask questions about those things that seem to lack explanation.

- Demonstrate an expectation to understand.

If the kids were going to be asking questions of the text anyway, I knew accessing books that spoke to social issues would invite a particular line of questioning that would allow us to explore issues of oppression. The texts I selected for this portion of our inquiry included titles such as Kristy Dempsey's *A Dance Like Starlight* (2014) and Zetta Elliott's *Milo's Museum* (2016). Each title was selected for its potential to help my group of seven- and eight-year olds openly question and explore acts of oppression while at the same time learn to be more intentional in their quest to read for meaning.

The first book, *A Dance Like Starlight*, tells the story of a young Black girl in the 1950s whose mother cleans and sews costumes at the Metropolitan Opera in New York City. Dreaming of one day becoming a ballerina herself, the heroine of the story attends the performance of Miss Janet Collins, the first Black prima ballerina to perform at the Met, and feels empowered by the power, beauty, and grace of Collins' performance on the stage. I stopped often during the story and asked the kids to share with a partner the questions that were developing in their minds as they listened, and then to build a discussion around these questions. At the end of the book the kids brought their questions and discussions back to the whole group (see Figure 5.5).

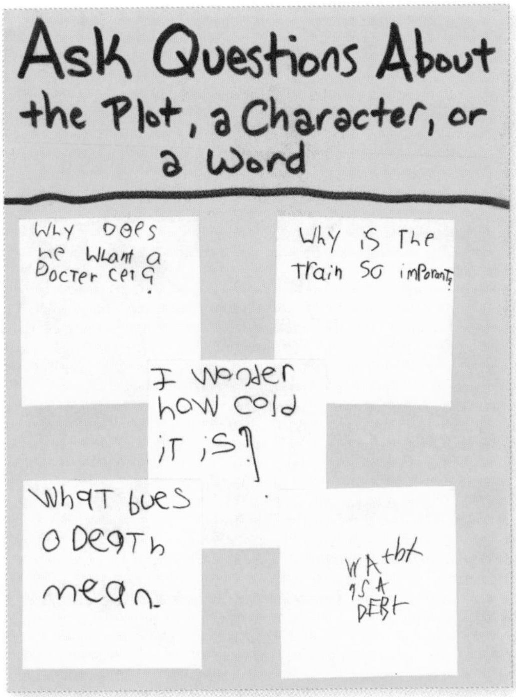

Figure 5.4

Student Questions in Response to Text

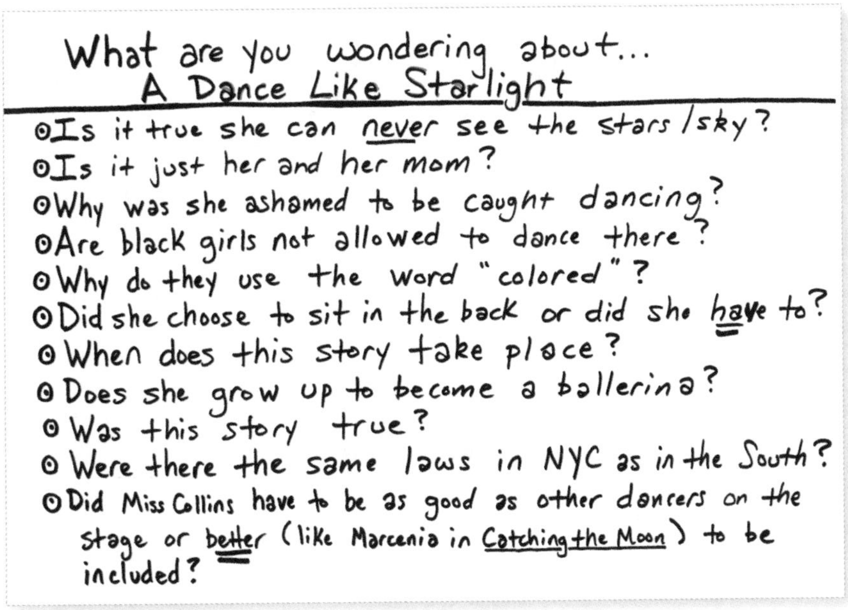

Figure 5.5

What Are You Wondering About?

Chris: So, what were some of the questions you were wondering about? Who wants to share a piece of the discussion you've been having with your partner?

Tiffany: Well, we were wondering why she sat in the back of the bus. Did she want to?

Chris: Why do you ask?

Tiffany: Well, we read that other book where the girl had to sit in the back—and her mother too. And she got in trouble for moving to the front.

Caleb: *The Bus Ride!*

Chris: OK, yeah. In the other book only white people could sit in front. They were in the South and there were laws about segregation—keeping people apart based on their race. Are you wondering if it's the same in this book?

Tiffany: Yeah, because maybe she couldn't sit in front.

Chris: OK, that makes me wonder whether the laws in New York City were the same, laws about segregation, as they were in the South.

Raleigh: I think she had to sit in the back. Is this story true?

Chris: What do you think?

Raleigh: I think it's true. When did it happen?

Chris: I don't think it's true, at least not all of it. But we could read the author's note to find out. When you look at the pictures and see the buildings and the cars and the people, can you get an idea of when this story was supposed to take place? Do you think it was in the past, in the present, or in the future?

Class: The past.

Kiersten: The cars look old. I wonder if she grew up to be a ballerina because she saw [Miss Collins] dance? Was this real?

Chris: Hmm, the author doesn't tell us that part of the story. I guess we're just supposed to imagine what we think would happen. No, I don't think the story is real but Miss Collins definitely was. She was a real dancer. She was the first Black woman to be a prima ballerina at the Met. That was a really big deal. But I wonder if she had to be better than all the other White dancers to get her chance to do this? Do you know what I mean? Not that she had to be incredibly good like other prima ballerinas but that she had to be *better* than all the rest to even get a shot.

Pierce: Like Marcenia. She didn't just have to be good at baseball to go to camp. She had to beat the boys.

Chris: Yeah, yeah, great connection. It's like *Catching the Moon* [Hubbard 2010]. It wasn't enough for Marcenia to be really good at baseball. Because she was a girl she had to prove herself even more than the boys did. She had to do something that's nearly impossible to do—steal home. The boys didn't. They had certain privileges Marcenia did not. People were more willing to believe boys would be good at baseball. Marcenia had to prove herself more because people didn't want to believe girls could be so good. I wonder if it was the same for Miss Collins because she was Black? Did the white prima ballerinas have certain privileges she didn't—like they had to be great but they didn't have to be the very best?

The selection of issue-based books for this part of our inquiry allowed the kids, with support, to begin questioning whether or not the world is fair to all people.

Goal 2: Using Issue-Based Texts to Help Students Gain Historical Context

In addition to using literature to better understand ourselves and others, carefully selecting from a broad range of multicultural texts provides opportunities for our students to gain the historical knowledge they need to make sense of current issues facing our communities. Without this contextual understanding, discussions about inequities tend to go nowhere because many assume this is "just the way things are." For instance, consider a question one of my students asked during Morning Meeting a few months into our third-grade year. Her question, one that gets asked most years, was in response to a book she'd been reading during independent reading the day before.

Elena: I was looking at a book yesterday and they had pictures of all the presidents. There weren't any girls. I was wondering, why isn't there any girl presidents?

Elena's question was a great demonstration of the type of careful observation and critical questioning that both defines and feeds so much of our work in the classroom. However, the ensuing discussion lacked any sort of productive analysis because the kids didn't possess enough historical context to accurately speak to the relationship between a male-dominated society and the underrepresentation of women in positions of power.

Jaylen: I think it's because girls don't really like to be president. I always see men doing it. Like, Barack Obama is a man.

Malik: Yeah but some women be the governor. Our governor is a woman. But I don't think she wants to be president.

Chris: You don't? What makes you believe Governor Haley doesn't want to be president?

Malik: I don't know. I just don't think she wants to be president.

Chris: Hmm, I'm not sure I agree. I mean, don't you think there are women who'd like to lead our nation? It sure seems like there must be.

Malia: Yeah, I'd want to be the president.

Other girls: Me too.

Jasmine: Well, I think it's just because they've been too busy doing other stuff. Maybe they'd like to be president but they just haven't done it yet.

When students lack personal experiences or adequate historical context to help them understand a particular injustice, they sometimes default to the belief the world is fair, assuming there must be a logical explanation capable of explaining away any sort of systemic injustice. In this case, Malik assumes females aren't interested in becoming president and Jasmine (a girl herself) declares females have just been too busy to even bother. To move classroom discussions toward social critique drawing on the relationship between power and oppression, teachers need to integrate literature into their curricular studies that provides students historical accounts speaking to these injustices. Only then can students access the past to better make sense of the present. For instance, books such as Tanya Lee Stone's *Who Says Women Can't Be Doctors: The Story of Elizabeth Blackwell* (2013), Susan Hood's *Shaking Things Up: 14 Young Women Who Changed the World* (2018), and Malala Yousafzai's *Malala's Magic Pencil* (2017) are all stories that could easily be incorporated into a variety of reading or social studies minilessons to meet the needs of curricular studies, while at the same time helping students begin to construct an understanding of all that has been denied women throughout history as well as efforts to change this.

We're fortunate to be teaching in a time when there is such an incredible amount of high-quality literature available to us. This is particularly true of both historical fiction and historical nonfiction. There's a wealth of titles offering glimpses into the lives, contributions, celebrations, and struggles of people from many walks of life. Figure 5.6 offers a sampling of such books. That said, large holes still remain. We're hard-pressed to locate many stories or accounts helping us understand what it has been like to experience 9/11 and its aftermath as a Muslim American, or reflect upon the historical experiences of those whose gender expression falls outside the expectations of the dominant culture. For this reason, we need to continue to push for more of these stories to be published.

Books That Provide Historical Context   Tool 🔧

Issue	Titles
Racial Discrimination/ Injustice	*Ruth and the Green Book* by C. Ramsey and G. Strauss *Harlem's Little Blackbird* by R. Watson *Let It Shine: Stories of Black Women Freedom Fighters* by A. Pinkney
Ethnic Discrimination/ Injustice	*Separate Is Never Equal* by D. Tonatiuh *Baseball Saved Us* by K. Mochizuki *I Am Not a Number* by J. K. Dupuis and K. Kacer
Religious Discrimination/ Injustice	*The Whispering Town* by J. Elvgren *Hidden* by L. Dauvillier *The World Is Not a Rectangle: A Portrait of Architect Zaha Hadid* by J. Winter
Gender Discrimination/ Injustice	*Ruth Bader Ginsberg: The Case of RBG vs. Inequality* by J. Winter *Elizabeth Leads the Way: Elizabeth Cady Stanton and the Right to Vote* by T. Stone *Ruby's Wish* by S. Bridges
Citizenship/ Immigration	*Mama's Nightingale: A Story of Immigration and Separation* by E. Danticat *Four Feet, Two Sandals* by K. Williams and K. Mohammed *My Journey with Papa* by D. Mills, A. Alva, and C. Navarro
War	*Brothers in Hope: The Story of the Lost Boys of Sudan* by M. Williams *The Librarian of Basra* by J. Winter *Faithful Elephants* by Y. Tsuchiya
Workers' Rights	*Brave Girl: Clara and the Shirtwaist Makers' Strike of 1909* by M. Markel *Which Side Are You On? The Story of a Song* by G. E. Lyon *Dolores Huerta: A Hero to Migrant Workers* by S. Warren

Figure 5.6
Books That Provide Historical Context

How to Integrate Historical Context into Our Curriculum

As we've already learned, social justice content integrates quite naturally into our literacy curriculum. But curricular integration need not stop there. We can implement social justice goals into other areas as well. For many, the most logical place to begin is social studies. Social studies serves as an ideal backdrop for helping students build cultural competence while also growing into critical thinkers. Figure 5.7 shares a second process for developing new studies (or even revising old ones) that allows us to meet the demands of our state standards while simultaneously teaching for social justice. The primary difference between this process and the one shared earlier is that we are no longer allowing the state standard to guide our teaching but instead placing our social justice work at the forefront. Once we've established what we hope to accomplish in the name of social justice teaching, then, and only then, do we identify which standards will be *uncovered* in the process.

To demonstrate what this looks like in action, I'll share a mini-inquiry my class and I conducted when launching our mandated third-grade social studies curriculum. I knew from past years this study of our state's history was heavily invested in teaching "whiteness as brightness," and marginalized social groups were often confined to small sections or even single pages. I wanted my students to learn to interrogate historical texts to determine whose histories were privileged and whose contributions were pushed to the margins. With this overarching topic in place, I next identified a social justice goal(s) best correlated with the work we would do. I chose:

- Help students become critical consumers of information.

 Tool

Process for Implementing Social Justice into Social Studies Curriculum

1. Identify the overarching topic of study.

2. Select social justice goal(s) to frame this inquiry.

3. Name specific outcomes for students.

4. Identify curricular standards that can be uncovered while in the process of this authentic work.

Figure 5.7

Process for Implementing Social Justice into Social Studies Curriculum

This was an obvious choice since the focus of our work would be to interrogate the nature of our social studies curriculum. Next, I named what it was I wanted to accomplish in very specific terms:

- Support students to question how history is written/made.

- Support students to analyze and evaluate historical accounts.

- Challenge students to identify the specific histories we need to seek out if we are to truly understand our state's history.

Finally, I identified the curricular standards that would be uncovered within this work.

Social Studies: Evaluate different forms of evidence used in historical inquiry and determine their validity.

Math: Collect, organize, classify, and interpret data with multiple categories and draw a scaled picture graph and a scaled bar graph to represent the data.

The outline for our mini-inquiry was framed as shown in Figure 5.8.

Imagining what this would look like in action, I knew above all I wanted my kids to become aware of the decisions historians make in regard to which stories are included and which are not. A critical reading of history, scrutinizing representation

1. **Identify the overarching topic of study.**	• Preview South Carolina state history.
2. **Select social justice goals to frame this inquiry (general).**	• Help students become critical consumers of information.
3. **Name specific outcomes for students (specific).**	• Question how history is written/made. • Analyze and evaluate historical accounts. • Challenge students to identify the specific histories we need to seek out if we are to truly understand our state's history.
4. **Identify curricular standards that can be uncovered while in the process of this authentic work.**	• *Social studies:* Evaluate different forms of evidence used in historical inquiry and determine their validity. • *Math:* Collect, organize, classify, and interpret data with multiple categories and draw a scaled picture graph and a scaled bar graph to represent the data.

Figure 5.8

Representation in South Carolina History Textbook Chapter

and the dissemination of one-dimensional accounts, is crucial because much of what our children receive from historical resources provided in schools privileges whiteness and maleness. This drowns out the value and contributions of all others. Sonia Nieto (2002) argues the inequitable selection of which histories get memorialized as well as the perspective from which these are told constitutes a "hidden curriculum" that supports the racial, ethnic, and patriarchal hierarchies plaguing our society.

Wanting to challenge this hierarchy, I split the kids into small groups and assigned each a chapter to preview. To learn how often men and women might be represented in this district-supplied text, I asked students to make a tally each time they saw a photo or illustration of a man or woman. When they finished, we came back together to share our data and discuss patterns we saw emerging.

Raleigh: I noticed there are a whole lot more pictures of men than women.

Ethan: Yeah, it's more than double.

William: It's more than triple.

Chris: Why do you think this is?

Tiffany: Probably because they don't think women have done important things.

Caleb: Yeah, like they haven't been mayor.

Chris: Not here in our city, no. But they've done lots of really important things. We know this because we learned about a lot of them last year when we invited all those people in to tell us about an important woman from our state who had inspired them in some way. Those women did such incredible things but may not even be in this book or in our state standards.

The next day we revisited the textbook chapters, but this time focused on representation by race. The kids then combined the numbers for each chapter and created bar graphs to represent their data. Again, large disparities were evident. I asked them to share what they noticed.

Eli'sha: I noticed that Native Americans are in Chapter 2 and 3 a lot and then they have a zero on all the other chapters.

Elizabeth: There weren't any pictures of them in those chapters at all. Just the first ones.

Kiersten: Same with Black people. Black people were mostly in just three chapters but not much in the others.

Ethan: Yeah, but white people were a lot in all the chapters except the one about Native Americans.

Chris: So what does this all mean?

Ethan: I think it means there's too much white people in this book and not enough of other people.

Kiersten: I think it means there should be more history stories about all the people.

Chris: OK, so what do you think we need to do then as we study our state's history this year? Where might we find these other important stories?

Engaging our kids in this work as historians allows them to work fluidly among multiple domains of social justice teaching. Students begin by developing a justice-oriented stance when critiquing historical texts to discover whose histories are centered and whose are placed at the margins, while at the same time identifying the role of author bias in determining which of these are included and which are excluded. Students are also positioned to take action alongside us as we seek out alternate accounts that provide a more holistic story of our past. In doing this work, students develop a greater understanding of how history is constructed—an understanding we hope follows them throughout their schooling and adulthood.

A Final Word of Caution About Incorporating Issue-Based Texts

When making efforts to introduce issue-based texts into our curriculum, it's critical we recognize the need to balance these stories of injustice with a larger collection of stories that simply normalize and celebrate our identities and diversity. Every book about Native Americans should not be ones depicting the struggles they've faced. Should we allow ourselves to fall into the trap of overusing issue-based texts, we run the risk of sending negative messages about marginalized groups of people. I can speak to this from personal experience. Many years ago, during a discussion about representation in children's literature, I was surprised to hear the following exchange between a handful of my non-Black students:

Chris: Seth, what did you want to say?

Seth: Well, I think there's a whole lot more books about Black people than back whenever there was special laws. But even though there's more books now than back then Black stories are, like, sad.

Margot: Hmm?

Seth: Like, for the Black people the stories are a lot of times sad but if you hear about white people the book is always so happy.

Chris: You're saying that the times when they have Black characters featured in the books they make these stories sad?

Colton: Yeah, like Ruby Bridges and all those others.

Adam: And in Mr. George Baker. He's a Black person and, well, it's sad. Building onto Noah, it's sad because he never learned how to read and he's a hundred years old.

Seth: Maybe because of schools back then. They weren't fair.

Adam: Yeah, maybe.

Chris: So, is your point that there aren't many stories about just fun families having a good time about Black people because the ones about Black people tend to be sad stories?

Seth: Yep.

Colton: Yeah, they're about freedom.

It's no exaggeration to say my heart sank directly into my stomach in that moment. After months of believing I'd helped my students become more enlightened to issues of injustice, it became clear I had, in fact, spent much of the year positioning Black children and their families as victims to be pitied—at least, those in print. This could have been avoided. This *should* have been avoided. But in truth I didn't know any better at the time. In my vigor to help students learn about oppression, I failed to recognize so many of the stories I'd read about the Black community focused on the collective struggles they face instead of the richness of their friendships, passions, and families.

We *must* strike a healthy balance when working to bolster our students' understanding of identity, diversity, and justice. It's not enough to teach only about injustice. That said, it's also not enough to teach only about love. Instead, we have to work in intentional ways to help our students develop empathy and gain historical context using issue-based texts, while at the same time developing positive social identities and celebrating diversity with a wide array of other texts. Each is absolutely essential.

Watch ▶

Why Issue-Based Literature Works:
Teacher Nozsa Tinsley explains why
literature is essential to her social justice
teaching.

**"Reading" a Commercial and the Media's
Response:** Chris Hass' students consider
how a commercial became a lightning rod
for many Americans' racism.

Placing Social Justice at the Core of Our Morning Meeting

Chris: All right, let's go ahead and get started with Morning Meeting. Who has a journal?

Colton: I do. I wrote a question in the Classroom Community Journal. It's about how we sit at lunch. Well, because there's this game we play at recess where a few boys and a few girls always play together. But at lunch boys and girls don't really sit by each other. I wonder why it changes at lunch.

Caitlin: Yeah, I noticed that, too. At lunch there's a boy table and a girl table.

Noah: I think I sort of know why boys and girls don't sit together. Because on the first day most boys were sitting at one table so all the other boys started sitting there. And then the girls probably didn't see much room so they had to sit at the other one. And so it started off like that and then it just stayed that way every day.

Malik: Well, I think we should stop with the boy table and the girl table because it's like two different tables that we sit in. And I don't even think the tables should be boy and girl.

Colton: But boys and girls are just at lunch. They're just sitting where they want to.

There are few things we can teach our students as important as learning to observe the world more closely and ask genuine questions about those things they feel lack adequate examination or explanation. If we can accomplish this, we will have helped our kids grow closer to becoming citizens capable of and willing to identify injustices at play in our society. But how do we help students begin to pay attention more carefully to the world around them? Or to question the status quo? And, where does this work fit within the flow of our already bustling school day?

In this chapter we'll learn to carve out time during our Morning Meeting to scaffold students into becoming social critics interested in making sense of the world they live in. In doing so, we'll work deliberately to help them observe the world more closely and begin questioning and critiquing all they see.

Repurposing Our Morning Meeting to Meet the Needs of Social Justice

For many, Morning Meeting is a time near the beginning of the day (Figure 6.1) when students typically sit in a circle on the floor, share something going on in their lives, engage in a short group activity or discussion, hear important announcements, and go over the agenda. Even with careful planning this can be a lot to accomplish in a relatively short amount of time. Still, a well-run Morning Meeting goes a long way in helping build strong relationships in our classrooms as we sit side by side and share our lives with one another.

Time	Structure/Subject
8:00–8:25	Explorations
8:25–8:55	Morning Meeting
8:55–10:45	Literacy Workshop
10:45–11:15	Lunch
11:15–11:30	Read-Aloud
11:30–12:20	Specials: Art, Music, PE, Computer, and Library
12:20–12:50	Recess
12:50–1:45	Math Workshop
1:45–2:35	Integrated Units of Study into Science and Social Studies
2:35–2:50	Read Aloud/Pack Up

Figure 6.1
Sample Daily Forecast

Given the conversational and open-ended nature of Morning Meeting, it's an ideal structure for implementing social justice work. In fact, I'll go one step further and argue the work we do in our Morning Meeting has the potential to lie at the very heart of our social justice teaching.

Basically, I will describe in this chapter a thirty-minute engagement where students, like Colton who wondered aloud about seating patterns in the lunchroom, share their burning questions with the class and then invite others to explore this topic with them. When you think about it, this work is closely related to what's already happening when we share issue-based texts in our classrooms as students openly express their questions, thoughts, and feelings.

A Morning Meeting dedicated to tackling issues of social justice mirrors this same process: students learn to pay close attention, reflect on what they see and hear, and then invite others to help them make sense of it all. The primary difference in our Morning Meeting is that a book is no longer the text our students are speaking back to—rather, the *world* is. When I refer to the world as a text (Freire 1970), I'm speaking to the fact we are constantly taking in information and creating meaning from all we see, hear, and feel in our everyday lives. Reading the world is the process by which we ultimately create our understanding of "reality." As such, Morning Meeting is essential because it bridges our kids' critical thinking from something that happens only in response to a shared text (a school practice) to something more generative that happens in response to the world they live in (a daily, life practice).

You might be thinking: *You're making this sound too simple. What if my kids just look at me with blank stares and have no questions to share? What if they don't notice a single thing?* Truth be told, this is likely. At least for a while. That's why we need to carefully structure this aspect of our Morning Meeting and provide lots of support along the way. This begins with the implementation of classroom journals.

Establishing Classroom Journals

Classroom journals, a practice adopted from my colleague Tim O'Keefe (Mills, O'Keefe, and Jennings 2004), play a key role in launching our mini-inquiries into issues of social justice during Morning Meeting. The journals—stapled booklets of eleven-by-seventeen-inch paper—provide a place where students can record and later present the questions, observations, and information they want their classmates to discuss. In our classroom, we have five journals in total: Science Journal, Language Journal, Math Journal, Classroom Community Journal, and Culture Journal (see Figure 6.2). When a student has an entry in mind they simply select the journal that best fits the content of their share (see Figures 6.3a and 6.3b). For instance, if they want to point out an issue that's developing in our classroom (say, people rushing to line up and pushing one another out of the way), they would place this concern in the Classroom Community Journal. However, if they're wondering why speed limits always end in a *0* or a *5*, they'd record this in the Math Journal.

Figure 6.2

Classroom Journals Spread Across
the Floor for Student Use

Figures 6.3a and 6.3b

Student Entries in the
Language (*left*) and
Science Journals (*right*)

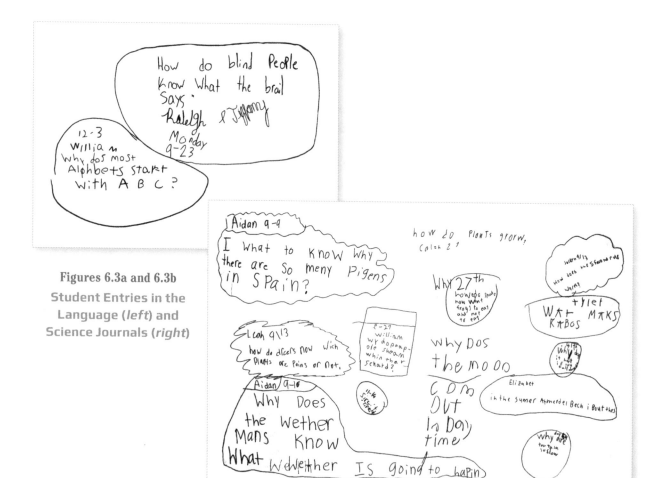

Although each of these journals supports students to develop a curiosity about the world around them and to continually ask questions about how things work, their entries in the Culture Journal primarily fuel our discussions around oppressive beliefs and practices (though entries in other journals, such as tensions in the Classroom Community Journal or statistics about representation in children's literature in the Math Journal, can also lead to justice-oriented discussions). The questions my students and I record in these journals constitute the curriculum of our Morning Meeting. Morning Meeting, then, is defined in our classroom as a structure where students circle up on the floor each morning not only to preview the day, share stories from their lives, and disseminate important information but also to discuss the burning questions emerging from their daily lives (see Figure 6.4).

To fuel Morning Meeting discussions around student inquiries, students are required to share at least one classroom journal entry with the class each month—although some opt to share much more often than this. The discussions that grow from these journals allow us to explore a wide variety of topics ranging from the lack of teachers of Color within our school to religious freedoms. That's not to say discussions running deep into the particulars of religion and race are present each

Math Journal

- Why is a clock a circle instead of a square?
- How many nanometers in a micrometer?
- I was watching a baseball game. The pitcher threw the ball 95 mph. I wonder how fast the hitter hit it.

Science Journal

- I wonder why sand dollars have lots of holes.
- How does the ocean refill?
- Why did extinct animals grow so big?
- How do monkeys clean their teeth?
- How do our bodies move?

Language Journal

- Why do we read left to right and not right to left?
- Why do some words sound the same but are not spelled the same so it's hard to know?
- Why do we say words but we don't know what they mean?

Culture Journal

- Why do people judge people by their skin color?
- Why do we need to go to school?
- Why do people like money and it's just paper?
- I wonder why girls dye their hair.
- Why in olden times women couldn't vote?

Classroom Community Journal

- Why when people have book recommendations they do it only for their friends?
- Why do people at our school bully?
- I hear some people in class say "But I didn't do anything. Someone else did it." Why do they blame someone else?

Figure 6.4

Sample of Student-Generated Questions in the Classroom Journals and every day, or even each and every week. Rather, these sorts of topics emerge at different times throughout the week, month, or year in response to something that's happened in the news, as the result of an observation, in response to a book or inquiry from other parts of our day, or from topics I've expressly brought to the circle in hopes of helping my students take notice of an issue. These are the discussions that fuel our social justice work. However, these questions rarely come easily to many kids. Most are just not used to being asked to think this way at school—to continually wonder about things that fall outside the limitations of a mandated curriculum. It becomes our role then to teach them to (re)discover a sense of wonder about the world.

(Re)discovering a sense of wonder

As classroom teachers we're surrounded each day by a roomful of wonderers whose questions are genuine and seemingly without limits. Yet, this may not always be so obvious because most students have learned that doing school well means suppressing such questions. Too often, classroom expectations call on them to do more sitting and listening than sharing—especially when the things they really want to know don't fit within the predetermined curriculum. Too many have been in classrooms where the teacher solely determines which questions guide classroom learning, how these questions will be explored, and, as a result, what specific meaning everyone will be expected to accept as truth at the end of it all.

We can change this. That said, it's not uncommon, when offering students an opportunity to share their curiosities and concerns, to find they aren't really sure what to do with such an invitation. Sure, when we ask them if they have a question connected to the particulars of an assignment they're working on, plenty of hands shoot into the air. But when we ask a more general question such as "So, what have you been wondering about lately?," we're often greeted by silence and uncertainty. Many, if not all, aren't sure what to make of this invitation. At least, not at first.

There are a couple of reasons for this. First, some are confused regarding what sorts of questions they're expected to ask. Adept at mastering the rules and expectations of schooling, some students fear asking the wrong kinds of questions when provided the incredibly open-ended nature of such an invitation. Because of this, they're more likely to sit back and wait until this new routine has been established to better understand the "rules" so they can be certain they're doing it "right." Second, some students become lost within the vast potential of options available to them when we say, "Share something with us that you're really curious about or that doesn't feel right to you." Our students don't always know where to begin. This tendency to feel overwhelmed is based on a theory in psychology known as the *paradox of choice*, which explains the more choices we have available to us the more anxiety we sometimes feel. Within the possibility of so many questions, students get lost trying to locate just one. And finally, some students struggle with the expectation to share their curiosities and concerns because, much like many adults, they've already begun to fall out of the practice of wondering about things. Instead, they tend to take it as it comes. Fortunately, once we've established a space in the classroom for their questions, there are a few simple steps we can take to support our students into posing the queries that will fuel rich classroom discussions.

Modeling how to question the world

One of the very first things we can do to scaffold students into the work of wondering is to offer our own questions as a model for what this work looks and sounds like. Often, for the first two or three weeks of the school year I am doing most, if not all, of the sharing. For instance, I might begin one of our first Morning Meetings with a question I've written in our Science Journal:

> Yesterday I heard that someone found a really big boa constrictor on the playground at one of the other schools near us. Oh my gosh, I wonder how it got there?! What do you think, how does a big boa constrictor wind up in a school yard?

Questions such as these excite children because they love nothing more than trying to come up with answers to questions that invite imaginative responses. The joy of sharing one's own thoughts while building knowledge alongside friends and peers makes for a highly engaging and pleasurable learning experience. Our questions, asked daily, provide the scaffold students need to begin seeing themselves as someone who could generate "I wonder" questions of their own. Figure 6.5 offers a sampling of the questions I've used in the past to model what this looks like as well as the sorts of guiding ideas one might use when generating their own questions.

Teacher-Generated Questions to Launch the Practice of Classroom Journals

Journal	Teacher Entry	Guiding Topics
Science	Yesterday I saw a worm that was torn in two pieces. I've heard people say both ends can grow into new worms. Is this true? What do you think?	Popular myth vs. reality
	On Sunday I saw a snake lying underneath a log in the woods near my house. I wonder why snakes usually lie underneath things. What do you think?	Animal behavior
	I noticed a red leaf on the ground this weekend. It's not even fall yet. I wonder why some leaves start changing colors so early (or so late).	Natural phenomena

(continues)

Teacher-Generated Questions to Launch the Practice of Classroom Journals

Journal	Teacher Entry	Guiding Topics
Math	I recently saw a graph showing who cooks on Mother's Day. Can you guess who cooks most often in celebration of this day? Why do you think this is?	Critical analysis of statistics
	Why do speed limit signs always end with a *5* or a *0*? Why not make the speed limit 62?	Math in the real world
Culture	I've noticed that my kids often want us to upgrade to the newest phone even though the ones we have still work fine. They don't know what makes the new phones any better than the old ones but they still believe they must be better. Why do we tend to believe things that are new (or more expensive) are better?	Social beliefs
	Why do some families often buy new clothes or new shoes at the beginning of the school year? I wouldn't think their old clothes are suddenly too small or worn out.	Social practices
	There are lots of magnet schools where all children are welcome but their parents have to drive them to and from school each day because there aren't buses available. I was wondering about the families who might love to send their kids to these magnet schools but can't because they have no way to get them there and back. What do you think about this?	Equity/fairness
Language	Someone in class was reading a book with the word *frenemy* in the title. At first I was wondering if this is a real word. Then I was wondering what even makes something a "real" word? If we use it, is that enough to make it real?	Social construction of language
	Some words seem to be really tricky to spell. Sometimes it's because two words are so similar and it's hard to remember which is which—like *where* and *were*, *their* and *there*, *which* and *witch*, and *to* and *too*. How might we learn to spell these?	Confusing nature of the English language
	We read a lot at my house. We read books, articles, instructions, maps, recipes, grocery lists, letters, and emails. What sorts of reading does your family do? Do you ever do it together?	Cultural practices/home practices

Teacher-Generated Questions to Launch the Practice of Classroom Journals

Journal	Teacher Entry	Guiding Topics
Classroom Community	What sorts of choices would you like for us to have during our exploration time each morning? What do you want to explore?	Inviting student input
	Later this morning we're going to do something fun in groups but I predict some groups will have trouble making decisions together. What sorts of problems do you sometimes have when working in a group? And can we think of some possible solutions?	Preemptive problem solving
	I've noticed we keep leaving our pencils out on the floor. A couple of people in class keep picking them all up on their own. That's really nice of them to do but I wonder what we could do differently to help everyone begin to clean up after themselves.	Addressing ongoing issues
	I've been noticing there are days when it looks like some people are alone at recess and unsure what to do. I imagine this happens to all of us at some point. I wonder, what could we do to make sure no one ever feels left out? What's our responsibility when we see this happening?	Supporting kids to take action

Figure 6.5

Teacher-Generated Questions to Launch the Practice of Classroom Journals

One of the beautiful things about our questions is that they not only support our kids into generating questions of their own but disrupt the notion that teachers have all the answers. By sharing our curiosities and tensions, students come to see us as people who are continually trying to make sense of things and who need their input in helping us figure these out. This is so important. Furthermore, demonstrating to our kids that we are forever wondering about the things we see helps our students view these journal entries as more than just an isolated classroom assignment but as supporting them to live their lives in a very particular way—continually questioning the logic, purpose, and workings of those things most people overlook or take for granted. Lastly, asking our own questions and then inviting students to step in and help us figure out the answers demonstrates the fact we all move in and out of teacher and learner roles while in the process of building new understandings together.

Generating questions alongside our students

In addition to asking our own questions throughout the year, we can also work with our kids to generate questions together. One way of doing this is to think aloud in front of them during whole-class engagements to demonstrate how questions grow out of our everyday experiences. In the following vignette I'm working with my second graders to demonstrate the fact there are many strategies available to them when adding numbers together.

Chris: OK, so the problem is eight plus five. We've already decided the sum is thirteen. That's fine but that's not the interesting part to me. What I'm most interested to find out is *how* you knew this. What did you do to add eight and five? Turn and talk with your neighbor about how you solved this. [*One minute of talk in partnerships*] All right, who'd like to share out? Peter?

Peter: Um, I, like, I started with eight and counted five more.

Chris: OK, how did you do that? How did you count five more?

Peter: I just held up five fingers and counted them.

Chris: Hmm, so Peter counted up from eight and he also used his fingers to help him do so. That makes sense. Who else? Who did something different? Jolina?

Jolina: Well, I saw eight plus five and so I did five plus five plus three and I got thirteen.

Chris: Wait, how did you get five plus five plus three out of this problem, eight plus five?

Jolina: Well, eight is really a five and a three so I added the two fives and then the three.

Chris: Oh, wow, you're right. We can totally do that! Hey, look at this everybody. Jolina took a tricky problem and made it simpler by breaking the eight into a five and a three—which makes eight. So you change the eight to a five and a three and then you can do the double, five plus five, and then add the three. Nice. Lots of ideas around the room. Who else?

Martin: I did it a little different.

Chris: Oh? How'd you do it, Martin?

Martin: I did eight tallies and then did five more and then counted them all.

Chris: OK, yeah, that totally works! Isn't it cool that we are all looking at the exact same problem but many of us are seeing it differently in regard to how we could solve it? I wonder how we learned all these different ways of doing math? Hey, that'd be a great question for the Math Journal: How did you learn to use different strategies when adding up numbers? I bet it comes from a lot of different places . . . but I'm not sure. I'd be interested to find out though. Would anyone like to add that to the Math Journal tomorrow morning and help us think more about how we learn all these strategies?

Allowing our students to see firsthand how daily conversation can lead to new questions the class may want to explore together is a powerful way of scaffolding students into the work of generating questions. These are rarely, if ever, planned in advance but emerge organically from the work we do in the classroom as readers, writers, mathematicians, scientists, and social scientists. These are true "Hey, I wonder . . ." moments. As we generate in-the-moment questions that grow out of the work we're doing with our students, we allow our kids to see how such questions take form so they can begin locating questions in their own daily interactions when watching a football game, shopping at the store, or hearing about something in the news.

Helping students take notice of the questions they're already wondering about

Another way to collaboratively construct questions with students is to listen carefully to the conversations they have with us and with their friends throughout the day and help them begin to recognize the potential of their thoughts for future questions. In such cases, we help our students recognize the fact they're already wondering about how things work and why they work the way they do. In the following vignette, Marshawn and I are walking around the track before school with a number of other students and we notice the geese that have congregated on the grass at the center of the track.

Marshawn: Look at all those geese over there.

Chris: I know, right? That's a lot of geese. I sure hope those kindergartners keep their distance because I'm not sure the geese are all that friendly.

Marshawn: They keep pecking.

Chris: Yeah, I noticed that too. They must see something in the grass.

Marshawn: What are they doing?

Chris: I don't know. It looks like maybe they're eating but I'm not sure.

Marshawn: What are they eating? Maybe worms?

Chris: Could be worms. Could be something else. I'm not real sure what geese eat.

Marshawn: Maybe worms and bugs.

Chris: Hmm, could be. I love how you're thinking about this because now I'm wondering about it too. I wonder if someone in class knows what geese eat when they're out in the grass like that. Hey, that'd be a great question for the Science Journal. You could tell people about seeing the geese pecking at the grass and ask them if they know what the geese might be eating. I'm sure a number of people would have some great thoughts.

Our kids wonder about things all the time—though they don't always take notice of this. As they quickly move their attention elsewhere, a good number of their wonderings become lost, as does the opportunity for mindful deliberation. Our goal, by naming the questions we see them pondering, is to help students learn to take notice of these moments of inquiry so they can explore their questions more fully as well as in the company of others.

Inviting families and caregivers to help generate questions

We can further support our students' questioning by inviting families and caregivers into the process of noticing the questions that emerge from their home life (see Figure 6.6). It's important to invite them into this work for a number of reasons. First, because some of the questions that wind up in our classroom journals are bound to make some families uncomfortable (particularly those challenging the unearned privileges particular groups hold within our society), inviting families to become part of the process of generating these questions allows them to play a role in our classroom discussions. Second, communicating the specifics of this work helps us earn their trust as we demonstrate the amount of thought and care we're putting into this structure. And finally, inviting families to help our students generate questions offers them additional support in transitioning into this "new" practice.

A week or two ago I received a photo via email from one of our classroom families that read "The boys wanted me to send you this picture." It showed two friends in the classroom holding a cool-looking cocoon (or was it a chrysalis?). I was so excited to get it because the boys knew I'd be *so* interested to see what they found. That, to me, is at the heart of what it means to be a classroom of inquiry—to live in wonder at the world around us and to share this joy of exploration and discovery with one another. When people ask me to define *inquiry*, I often try to explain it as (1) constantly questioning, (2) learning *how* to learn, and (3) critiquing what it is we are learning. Questions are at the heart of all we do.

Many of our studies are rooted in wonderings that begin "I wonder . . . ," "Why . . . ," "What . . . ," and so on. Because many of the questions come directly from the kids, much of what we learn is negotiated. We learn the things the state says we need to know but we also explore the curiosities and interests of the kids. It's not worksheets or textbook pages or lectures that help kids learn; rather, it's questions, explorations, careful observations, research, discussions, and critique. More often than not, these lead us to a whole new set of questions.

A wonderful part of our school day is our Morning Meeting. This is when the kids share so many amazing questions with us in our classroom journals. This structure helps support the kids into a questioning sort of life

and allows us time to think about all sorts of things that otherwise we might never have thought to address. Here's a sampling of questions and observations the kids have offered so far this year.

From Our Math Journal

I ask my parents to mark my height against the wall every two or three months. I like to mark my height to see how much I have grown. When my Dad measured the marks we noticed a few things. I have grown 5 inches since starting kindergarten. I was 44 inches and now I am 49. Another cool thing I am 9 inches taller than my little brother but I am 21 inches shorter than my dad.

From Our Language Journal

How do babies learn to talk?

From Our Science Journal

Why do giraffes have a purple tongue?

From Our Culture Journal

Why are there bullies? Why can't they all be friends?

When you're chatting with your children at home and you come across a really good question about something you'd both like to better understand, send it in with them. We'd love to see those questions make it into our

Figure 6.6

Excerpt from Classroom Newsletter

Despite these efforts, the end of each month inevitably finds a small handful of students who have yet to share a question with us during Morning Meeting. For various reasons, they've not taken up the questions that have emerged from our whole-group work or those I've named back to them when listening to them talk. I sit alongside these students during our explorations time and shrink the possibilities down to allow them to more easily locate the things they don't understand just yet but would like to. For instance, I might say:

> So, we've been working with electricity a lot lately. We've been trying to figure out how to build different types of circuits. Some of our attempts have made the light bulb light up and others haven't been so successful. I wonder, as you've been working with electricity, has there been anything you didn't quite understand or something you'd like to know more about? It might have been about the circuits or maybe it was about something to do with electricity in general. Tell me, what have you been wondering about electricity?

There are times when it feels incredibly challenging to help our children think a little deeper about their own understanding and to question the tensions they encounter in their learning and in their everyday lives. But despite the challenge, this work is absolutely essential because if we're to create classrooms of critical thinkers, we must do everything in our power to help our students begin taking notice of those things, no matter how small, that don't make sense to them. If we're to help them learn to build rich discussions rooted in exploratory talk or to critique the merit of new information, it must become second nature for our children to take notice when things don't quite add up. And as we help them begin to question, we can simultaneously work to broaden their horizons from questions about math, literacy, and science to questions challenging the passive acceptance of oppressive beliefs and practices.

Starting Social Critique with Gender

You probably won't be surprised to find that as our class discussions progress over the course of the year, those students from marginalized populations have many personal stories, concerns, and frustrations to share in regard to how they're sometimes misrepresented or mistreated by society, and students from the dominant culture (white, male, Christian, etc.) often fail to understand where these feelings are coming from, given the stories and accusations they're hearing don't at all reflect their own personal lived experiences. Although I always invite such stories as soon as students are ready to share them, I choose to focus social critique on questions that are more comfortable and accessible to all students—at least at first. I ease my students into thinking critically about social beliefs and practices by first asking questions that deal with topics they've all experienced and that feel more comfortable to them in that moment. Of course, what constitutes familiar or "comfortable" is going to be different from one class to another. I've found that in my classroom, gender is often a great place to begin.

Once I've established classroom journals as a daily practice, I begin to focus heavily on the Culture Journal when asking my own questions. Conveniently, it doesn't take long for me to overhear a gendered or sexist comment I can use to launch a classroom discussion. For instance, when provided materials to choose from such as markers or construction paper, I inevitably hear someone giggle and comment about a boy choosing a "girl color." Often, someone comes to this boy's defense and argues there is no such thing as boy colors and girl colors. Others step in to voice their own opinions. The stage is set.

Situations like this one offer firsthand, shared experiences that allow us to explore gender-related beliefs. For instance, I might use this classroom experience to launch a discussion about societal beliefs.

> I've written something in the Culture Journal. It reads, "Yesterday I heard a discussion in class about whether or not pink is a girl color. Some people felt it is while others said there's no such thing as girl colors. I was feeling a little confused because this is a topic I've heard come up quite a lot over the years. I'm wondering, *are* there such things as girl colors and boy colors?"

There are two important points I'd like to stress regarding an entry such as this. One is that although we may discuss behaviors or beliefs we encounter in our daily lives, my students and I never provide the names of those involved or talk about the ideas of others in a judgmental way that might threaten their standing as a caring friend in the classroom. Rather, we're grateful for the opportunity to think more deliberately about where our beliefs come from and the effect they have on ourselves and others. The second point I want to stress is that the goal of such discussions is not necessarily to come to a final conclusion about gendered colors (though the class often does on this particular question) but to use this question as an opportunity, over the course of a day, a week, or a year, to begin asking subsequent questions such as:

> Why do people believe there are boy colors and girl colors? Where did they learn this?
>
> Have people always believed in boy and girl colors? If not, when and why did this belief emerge?
>
> If people made this up, does that mean it's not real? Can it be changed? Should it be changed?
>
> What do the differences in "boy colors" and "girl colors" say about how we view girls?

What does it say about how we view boys? Is this important?

Are we part of the process of passing on this belief to others?

Do we see anyone in our lives or in the world who disrupts this belief in any way?

Now that we've thought more about this, how might we live our lives differently than we did before?

There is often a great deal of disagreement when discussing these questions. Each child accesses their individual experiences and desires when making sense of the issue at hand. Inevitably, this leads to conflict. The beauty of this work, however, is that it offers us opportunities to help our students learn how to successfully navigate conflict while ensuring others in the room have the opportunity to learn from—or at least process and critique—multiple perspectives.

Provided this, we can draw on these experiences to establish a launching point from which to begin thinking critically about social beliefs and practices—such as the use of terms like "tomboy" (see a breakdown of this discussion in Figure 6.7). In creating opportunities and outlets for our students to begin identifying those things that make them feel uncomfortable, confused, or upset, we begin the process of supporting them into social critique.

Elevating the Quality of Discussions

Once students begin questioning the world, our next step is to help them elevate the quality of their discussions. In the first few months of the school year my students' ability to engage in critical discussions doesn't come easily. These aren't discussions they're used to having in the classroom. For most, these aren't discussions they're used to having anywhere. From inexperience critiquing how the world works to a reluctance to share partial understandings in front of their peers, there are many challenges to consider. Yet we can help them get there.

One key aspect of this work is to ensure everyone is invested in listening and learning—including us. Too often we allow ourselves to dominate discussions, acting as though the primary role of the teacher is to pass along the whole of their unquestioned wisdom. But we can accomplish much more when we learn to restrain ourselves from such an approach. It's when we learn to simply listen that our kids' voices—and by extension, their ability to think both collaboratively and critically—begin to emerge. And as we refrain from dominating discussions, the rechanneling of our "sage on the stage" energy can instead be invested into more productive outlets, such as observational notetaking to track patterns in our students' participation (see Figure 6.8).

Key Components of Justice-Oriented Discussions

Chris: Who says there are tomboys? Who says there aren't? Where have you heard this before?

Imani: Well, my mom says I act like a tomboy sometimes but Elena said yesterday there is no such thing as a tomboy.   ← Contrasting Viewpoints

Elena: Yeah, there's not.

Chris: Why do you say that, Elena?

Elena: Because some girls like to play with dolls and stuff. Some don't, like me. It doesn't matter. And why is it called "tom"?

Malik: Well, it's probably because they don't like the color pink and the girl stuff. They probably like the boy stuff like Legos and Ninjago and Ninja Turtles.

Briana: No, that's not boy stuff. Who said that was boy stuff, Malik? Because I know lots of girls who like to play with Legos.   ← Students as Primary Resources

Malik: Oh, well . . .

Contrasting Viewpoints: One of the most powerful aspects of these discussions is the opportunity for students to realize the contested nature of beliefs too many blindly adopt. At times, this means questioning logic we've learned at home. As you might expect, this takes some careful maneuvering. My approach to this inevitable aspect of social justice work is to consistently communicate to parents (often through a class newsletter) our dedication to learning how to listen carefully to one another, to understand there are times we will not always agree, and to handle these sorts of exploratory discussions with respect and commitment to learning from others.

Students as Primary Resources: Because we want our students to become critical thinkers, we must help them more carefully consider how it is they've come to form their beliefs—especially about things they have no personal experience or firsthand knowledge of. One way to accomplish this is to ensure those who *do* have firsthand knowledge (such as Briana when speaking to whether or not girls like to play with Legos) have an opportunity to address the misunderstandings or oppressive beliefs of others.

Figure 6.7
Key Components of Justice-Oriented Discussions

	News	Journal	Participation (Hand raised or speak)	Notes (Reflection on this month)
1 William	Surfers rescue drowning man	(SCI) How did Big Bang begin?	||| (spaces out often)	Need reminders & helpful article to summarize to make sense
2 Abby	Overweight cat	(SCI) Why can't we see plants grow?		HH HH	Much more participatory!
3 Caleb	Football - pressure to gain weight	(SCI) How technology improve?	HH HH	Not called on often enough by peers.
4 Elizabeth	Boy finds fossilized tooth	(CC) People talk over others	||||	Wants to talk - not sure what to say & target
5 Tyler	USC football	(C) Why did people kill Jesus?		struggled to think of journal or find article
6 Aidan	Giving Tuesday	(C) Why no school on weekends?	|||	Mom helped w/ article
7 Brooklyn	Lantern flies	(C) Why do we have money?	||	Hesitant to share
8 Raleigh	Harriet Tubman on 20 bill	(C) Why Daylight savings time?	HH HH HH||	very willing to take risks in responses
9 Tiffany	Gender fluid dolls	(C) Cheating at recess	HH HH HH HH || HH HH HH HH HH	Constantly listening & responding
10 Leah	Library for homeless	(C) Why age limits on games?	HH		More participatory - but need more!
11 Jonah	Koala thinks dog is mother	(SCI) How turtles?	||	Daydreams consistently, mom helped w/ article
12 Isaac	Adults using TikTok	(SCI) Why are there cockroaches?			Need to invite into disc, move
13 Pierce	Wildlife killed at road crossings	(SCI) Why are drinks colored	HH HH HH HH	Responses more and more thoughtful and productive to disc.
14 James	New playstation	(SCI) Why round Earth not flat?	HH	Attentive, but not talking much
15 Zeina	Down Syndrome model Am. Girl		|||	Daydreams often
16 Joseph	Komodo Island, Protecting dragons	(SCI) run fast?	||||	Attentive, not talking much
17 Ethan	Poison bugs Caterpillars	(SCI) open everything?	HH HH HH HH HH	Very active, participates, talks over others
18 Eli'sha	Space Camp and Army	(SCI) Why feet fog?	HH HH HH HH HH	Hot & cold - with us or not
19 Maya	Young people making difference	(CC) water in bathroom	HH HH HH HH HH	Critical thinking on the regular - asks tough questions of others
20 Andrew	Scientists find fastest ant	(C) Why take food on commercials?	HH HH HH |||	Talks often but not always on topic
21 Jordyn	Overweight cat	(SCI) How ingredients mix together?	||	?
22 Kiersten	Cat changes outcome of game	(C) Dad helped homeless man	HH HH HH HH |||	Leader - consistently raising level of discussions

SCI HH HH HH |||| (19)
C HH HH (10)
CC HH ||| (8)
M (0)
L || (2)

Figure 6.8

Sample Kidwatching Notes

In this section I will describe generative ways we can support students to elevate the quality of their discussions. These include: (1) positioning students as the primary meaning makers in the classroom, (2) supporting students to listen closely, (3) scaffolding students to build onto the ideas of others, and (4) teaching students to value the role of disagreement within exploratory discussions.

Positioning Students as Primary Meaning Makers

I often think of my role within our Morning Meeting as teaching from the side. "Teach from the side" means to step out from the spotlight and position myself as an experienced and knowledgeable peer alongside my kids as they work to do much of the heavy lifting involved in their learning. Within the Morning Meeting, this means slowly and carefully releasing the responsibility for the discussion and meaning making to my students while still carefully stepping in, when needed, to nudge the discussion along, provide contextual information, and offer competing perspectives (see Figure 6.9).

Teacher-Centered Discussions →	Transitional Discussions →	Student-Centered Discussions
Teacher advances the discussion.	Teacher prompts student posing the question to advance the discussion. "Nic, do you want to call on someone else?"	Student posing question advances the discussion.
Teacher is primary audience for students' responses.	Teacher prompts students to speak to one another. "Be sure to look at your classmates, and not me, when you're speaking. They're your audience. They're primarily the ones you're building this discussion with."	Peers are primary audience for students' responses.
Teacher asks follow-up questions to draw out more information.	Teacher prompts students to request more information when they're not certain they fully understand an idea that's been shared. "Does anyone have any questions about what they just heard? Do you have a follow-up question you might want to ask Imani?"	Students ask follow-up questions to draw out more information.
Teacher challenges ideas that lack logic, reason, or credibility.	Teacher prompts students to challenge ideas that lack logic, reason, or credibility. "Do you all agree? Can someone offer a different perspective on this?"	Students challenge ideas that lack logic, reason, or credibility.
Teacher makes connections between the discussion topic and students' own personal experiences.	Teacher prompts students to make a connection between the discussion topic and their own personal experiences. "Does anyone have a connection to this? Maybe you've experienced something similar in your own life?"	Students make connections between the discussion topic and their own personal experiences.
Teacher often gets final word within the discussion.	Teacher prompts students to offer a final word. "Thinking about all the ideas that've been shared, what do you think, Colton? What are some of the big ideas you think we'll want to hold onto or keep thinking about?"	Students often get final word within the discussion.

Figure 6.9
Gradual Release of Responsibility in Classroom Discussions

At first, restructuring the relationships of power within classroom discussions can feel awkward. As teachers we're used to not only leading these discussions but, oftentimes, doing the bulk of the talking. Yet, we need to reconsider the stronghold we've long maintained as *the* voice in classroom discussions. We have to recognize that positioning our students as receivers of knowledge, as opposed to creators of knowledge, has a negative impact on our students' identities as learners as well as their relationships to learning. Students quickly learn there's little value in trying to figure something out if the teacher will ultimately swoop in to set things straight and provide the "real" knowledge at the end.

When we do more listening and less talking, we see our students genuinely begin to engage in these discussions—moving in and out of teacher and learner roles alongside their peers. Each of their thoughts, concerns, and questions work in concert with the contributions of others to provide pathways for new inquiries and learning. Speaking to the generative benefits of helping students do this work, Peter Johnston (2004) writes, "The more we help children build a sense of themselves as inquirers and problem-solvers . . . the more they are likely to transfer their learning into the world beyond school." This is our aim—to build practices that support our kids to transfer their social justice work in the classroom into the world beyond school. We can do this when implementing specific teaching moves (see Figure 6.10) to position our students as the primary meaning makers in these discussions.

To illustrate, I'll share another of our Morning Meeting discussions. In this vignette, it's early in our second-grade year and I'm taking a very active role within the discussion in hopes of establishing expectations as to how whole-group discussions will work over the course of the school year. Elena has placed a question in the Culture Journal that grew from a connection she'd made the day before during a discussion about the differences between Halloween costumes marketed to girls and those marketed to boys. In the earlier discussion Elena had noted that stores often sort toys, like Halloween costumes, by gender.

Elena: I have the Culture Journal. Why do they have boy aisles and girl aisles for toys at the store?

Chris: Hmm. Good question. Everyone take a moment to think about that. Does it make sense to you to have boy aisles and girl aisles in the toy section? I'm excited to think about this because I've noticed that too. I wonder why we do this. What do you all think? [*Ten second pause for kids to think*] Take a moment and turn to your circle buddy to tell them what you're thinking and then Elena can help us discuss it.

[*The kids take about a minute to build conversations with an assigned carpet partner.*]

Chris: So, what'd you all think? Elena, this is your discussion. Why don't you get us started.

Elena: Well, I think that it's OK if people go in different places because I like the boy section a lot and it could just be together.

Chris: Are you saying you wish all the toys could be together in a kids' section instead of broken up into a boy and girl section?

Elena: Yeah, I think that people like different things.

Peter: Well, sometimes I have to play with girl toys because when I go to my dad's house I have to play with my little sister.

Chris: What makes it a girl's toy again?

Peter: Well . . .

Chris: You just said you have to play with a girl toy, so I'm just wondering what makes it a girl toy.

Kumail: He thinks the *thing* is a girl's toy. But there *is* no girl toys.

Chris: Well, we can say that but sometimes we might catch ourselves thinking it—in terms of boy toys and girl toys. Probably all of us are guilty of doing it at least sometimes. Don't you think?

Malik: My dad thinks there are girl toys. He likes for me to play with boy toys because he's in the Army.

Peter: Do you play with [girl toys]?

Malik: No, I don't like girl stuff like making bracelets.

Alex: Hey, I like that stuff!

Chris: Ha, I love how Malik and Alex both have specific examples of this from their homes and can share those stories with us to help us understand how toys work at their house. Sometimes we disagree. Sometimes we see it differently.

Laila: I was just wondering why boys don't play with Barbie dolls and they're usually pink but the boys' stuff is blue and green.

Chris: Those are good questions. Laila has noticed it's not just toys that are considered to be specifically for boys or girls but sometimes it's colors too. Great connection, Laila.

Noah: Well, my sister, me, and my little brother all love to play with the tiny Hot Wheels cars and they're in more of a boy color, but my sister still likes them anyway because there's no boy or girl toys.

Chris: I'm prone to agree with you, Noah, but I also want to think about this some more. It's a good question, Elena. These are the sorts of beliefs—that there are toys only for girls or toys only for boys—we should really question and talk about. Maybe sometimes the way things are don't make a lot of sense to us and we want to know why people believe in it. We want to consider whether or not we believe in it. It's the difference between accepting that something is true and saying instead, "No, I need to figure this out for myself." Thanks for the discussion, Elena. Who else has a journal today?

 Tool Teaching Moves for Morning Meeting

Teaching Move: Modeling the fact that adults do not have all the answers

What This Means

Students are often taught to direct their responses toward the teacher in hopes of receiving a verbal or nonverbal cue that assures them they have answered a given question correctly. Within this common practice, the adult is positioned as the keeper of knowledge while students are positioned as being void of knowledge until their understanding of a topic matches that of the teacher. Teaching in this way not only negates the wealth of information, experiences, and views students bring with them to the classroom but also vastly privileges the teacher's knowledge.

Within a discussion, this causes students to continually speak *at* the teacher, rather than *with* their peers. Instead, we want our students to engage in dialogue with all members of the classroom to collaboratively build new knowledge. When we show our students that we do not already have the answers to all their questions, we invite them to become part of the process of negotiating new knowledge alongside us. In doing so, we invite them to become our teachers.

What It Looks Like

Chris: Hmm. Good question. Everyone take a moment to think about that. Does it make sense to you to have boy aisles and girl aisles in the toy section? I'm excited to think about this because I've noticed that too. I wonder why we do this?

Instead of taking a position of authority over Elena's question I let students know that I, too, am excited to think about this question and think aloud to myself, "I wonder why we do this?"

Teaching Moves for Morning Meeting

Teaching Move: Demonstrating the tentative nature of knowledge

What This Means

Too often students believe there is a simple, easily defined answer to every question. For many of the questions they ask about the natural world, this is true. But when we venture into questions about the beliefs and practices present within a culture, simple solutions often evade us as we learn that people experience the world differently. The social problems we encounter within a society are often the product of a wide range of factors working in concert. For this reason, we need to model for our students that we are always looking to learn more about these issues and to hear from many different people.

Within a discussion, helping students see that our knowledge is always incomplete around these issues helps give value to the fact we need to engage in an ongoing inquiry where many voices are heard. This accomplishes two goals within our discussions. The first is to disrupt the common challenge, "We've already talked about this." The second is to demonstrate the need for all voices to be heard over time to inform us of their own experiences and thoughts.

What It Looks Like

Chris: I'm prone to agree with you Noah but I also want to think about this some more.

There will be times when we feel it necessary to take a firm position on a particular belief—such as the need to treat others with love, compassion, and respect. But there are other times, such as here, when it benefits our kids to see that we feel a need to reflect on this more or to continue to seek out more information in hopes of better understanding an issue.

Teaching Move: Positioning students as ones who would know or have an idea

What This Means

A portion of our students are often very quiet, especially within discussions of topics they have not spent much time considering. These students may feel as though they have nothing to share or are concerned their thoughts are not as well informed as those of others in the classroom.

Within a discussion, this fear of having nothing of value to share causes some students to become passive members of the group, which feeds their lack of agency while at the same time robs the discussion of their valuable knowledge and perspective. Our goal in positioning students as ones who *would* have a thought on these topics is to challenge them to construct new identities for themselves as both agentive teachers and learners.

What It Looks Like

Chris: Hmm. Good question. Everyone take a moment to think about that. Does it make sense to you to have boy aisles and girl aisles in the toy section? . . . What do you all think? Take a moment and turn to a partner and tell them what you're thinking, and then Elena can help us discuss it.

Rather than asking a question such as "Does anyone have a response to this?," prompts such as "Does it make sense to you . . . ," "What do you all think?," and "Turn to a partner and tell them what you're thinking" position all students as active participants who *will* have something to share.

(continues)

Teaching Moves for Morning Meeting

Teaching Move: Acknowledging and giving weight to a wide range of student responses

What This Means

Because not all of our students are accustomed to questioning social beliefs and practices, many are hesitant to speak with much confidence on these topics. They fear saying something that might not be true or might be rejected by their peers. However, just as we work in our math workshop to help students learn to become risk takers who are willing to celebrate approximations when exploring new concepts and strategies, we must do the same in our Morning Meeting discussions.

This means that within a discussion, we work to make our students feel valued when being brave enough to share their tentative understandings with the class as points of departure for further conversation.

What It Looks Like

Malik: My dad thinks there are girl toys. He likes for me to play with boy toys because he's in the Army.

Peter: Do you play with [girl toys]?

Malik: No, I don't like girl stuff like making bracelets.

Alex: Hey, I like that stuff!

Chris: Ha, I love how Malik and Alex both have specific examples of this from their homes and can share those stories with us to help us understand how toys work at their house. Sometimes we disagree. Sometimes we see it differently.

After Malik offers a differing perspective to the question of gendered toys, he and Alex fall into a brief conflict over the value of making bracelets. I quickly step in to give value to their contributions by stating I love how they each provided specific examples.

Teaching Move: Helping to clarify or reframe student responses

What This Means

There are students who at times struggle to speak clearly or directly to the topic at hand. This may be because their understanding is incomplete or it may be because they do not yet have the words to effectively communicate the complex thoughts swirling around their heads.

Within a discussion, a fear of not being understood or not being directly on topic can quickly dissuade students from sharing their developing understandings with the group. For this reason, our job becomes to clarify or reframe their statements in a way that communicates, as accurately as possible, their intent, or pulls the general nature of their idea back to the topic at hand. Our goal is to help them feel the power of sharing ideas that contribute to the process of meaning making for the whole class.

What It Looks Like

Malik: My dad thinks there are girl toys. He likes for me to play with boy toys because he's in the Army.

Peter: Do you play with [girl toys]?

Malik: No, I don't like girl stuff like making bracelets.

Alex: Hey, I like that stuff!

Chris: Ha, I love how Malik and Alex both have specific examples of this from their homes and can share those stories with us to help us understand how toys work at their house. Sometimes we disagree. Sometimes we see it differently.

I reframe Malik and Alex's conflict in a positive way by stating they were helping us understand the issue in relation to each of their home practices.

Teaching Move: Selectively positioning our own contributions

What This Means

Perhaps the biggest barrier in attempting to help students move in and out of leadership roles within these discussions is their tendency to defer to us. Often, when students are asked to reflect on a question, text, or problem, the responses they produce are followed by *the* answer from the teacher. As teachers, we often have the final word and use this as an opportunity to set everything straight or share an ultimate truth that was missed or misrepresented by our students. At times this is necessary. However, by doing so on a regular basis we teach our students that the meanings they create are not only less valuable but serve as mere placeholders until the teacher provides the knowledge that will be valued and taken up as truth.

Within a discussion, it is critical that teachers be ever mindful of how often they speak, when and how they enter the discussion, and what they hope to accomplish with their words. Within the context of helping students move in and out of teacher and learner roles, it is imperative to avoid being the definitive voice at the end of every discussion.

What It Looks Like

Chris: I'm prone to agree with you, Noah, but I also want to think about this some more. It's a good question, Elena. These are the sorts of beliefs—that there are toys only for girls or toys only for boys—we should really question and talk about. Maybe sometimes the way things are doesn't make a lot of sense to us and we want to know why people believe in it. We want to consider whether or not we believe in it.

Though I am the last one to speak within the discussion, my closing contribution does not provide a final decision on why we have gendered toy aisles or even whether or not this practice is right or wrong. Rather, I use these final words to applaud the question Elena has brought to the group as well as to show value for the critical thinking this type of question demands of us.

Figure 6.10
Teaching Moves for Morning Meeting

Supporting Students to Listen Closely

Also vital to quality classroom discussion are our students' willingness and ability to listen closely to others. In my experience working with younger children, this skill often takes a great deal of time and patience to develop. For instance, one year I asked my new group of students to go home and have written conversations (see Figure 6.11) with their families speaking to why they think we go to school. I imagined this would be a wonderful opportunity to bring perspectives from home into the classroom while also setting the stage for all I hoped to accomplish over the course of the coming year.

When my kids returned the following morning, I asked them to take some time revisiting these conversations and then share out what they and their families felt

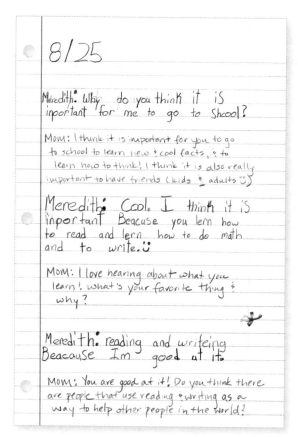

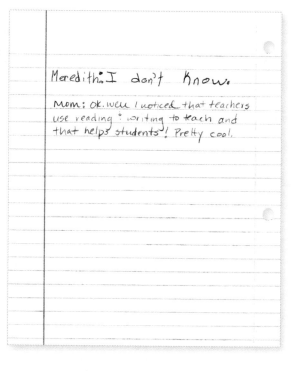

Figure 6.11

Written Conversation Discussing Reasons We Go to School

was most important about school. Not so surprising, given the fact this was the beginning of the year, the attempted discussion that followed was superficial at best. I later wrote in my teaching journal:

> The ideas the kids shared today about why we go to school were really interesting. Lots of parents spoke to the need to prepare for college or jobs. Others spoke to the role of education in helping our communities. But in regard to establishing our Morning Meeting, more important than what was said today was how the kids heard it—or in this case, didn't hear it. They paid such little attention to each other and showed hardly any interest at all in other people's ideas. To be honest, this is consistent with many other parts of our day right now. They know how to behave in the circle but they're not demonstrating a readiness to truly listen to anyone other than me. It's crucial for them to learn to listen, think, and respond in meaningful ways to their friends around the room. I'm realizing more and more that certain things have to be in place before we can explore topics such as power, race, normalcy, gender, etc. We have to learn to engage with ideas as well as with one another. In terms of what I hope we can accomplish this year, this ability to listen to one another must come first.

Although learning to listen closely to others and build on their ideas are skills we take up across many curricular structures, Morning Meeting serves as a particularly effective means of helping students come to understand the power of collaborative thinking within the large group. These discussions offer us a daily opportunity to communicate clear expectations for what it means to actively listen to the thoughts of others.

As with other types of learning that take place in our classroom, the skill of listening closely is often taught through the process of noticing and naming. Just as we access mentor writers in writing workshop to uncover the craft moves our favorite authors make, give these names, and then attempt to employ them in our own writing, we can call attention to the ways of being that enable classmates to become better listeners as well. For example, two weeks after the less-than-successful discussion about why we go to school, my second-grade class turned a corner. A question Sophie wrote in the Science Journal about drinking water served as our entry point. I later reflected in my journal:

> Today Sophie shared something in the Science Journal. She asked why it is we drink so much water. This seemed like a rather obvious question, even to the kids in the circle. However, the coolest thing happened. Elena said we drink water to stay hydrated, then Silas added to her idea by saying this is especially the case after recess when they all come in hot from the playground. Braden added they are also very sweaty, to which I pointed out sweating keeps us cool but probably accelerates the process of dehydration since we are losing liquids from our body. Chase finished the discussion by pointing out we need to stay hydrated to stay alive. I loved this discussion because it was the first time I heard the kids building onto the ideas of others. Each person who shared something pushed our understanding of water, hydration, and life one step further. This was such a perfect example of co-constructing knowledge. One person's idea led another to think of something else.

Following this short discussion about water consumption and hydration, I immediately named for my students what I noticed them doing to make this such a rich discussion.

Chris: I want to take a moment and call attention to something really cool I just noticed about Sophie's discussion. Sometimes in the past I've noticed that when people share in the circle, others are wiggling around and not always paying much attention. But just now we did something really cool. Sophie asked her question, Elena shared a thought, then a whole bunch of people—me included—listened closely to what others had to say and added onto their thoughts. We listened carefully, then added more information to help us understand why we drink so much water. If we weren't such good listeners, we couldn't have learned all the stuff we just did. It's so cool how we figured this out together. Tell me, when you look around the circle during Morning Meeting, how can you tell when someone is really listening closely to the ideas others are sharing? What do you think this kind of careful listening looks like?

Noticing and naming the behaviors that promote careful listening provides students well-defined expectations for classroom discussions (see Figures 6.12 and 6.13). Students learn to take notice of these behaviors and live into them on an increasingly consistent basis.

Another key to helping students become better listeners during class discussion is to make certain they have many opportunities to share their thinking. Once students notice that only a small handful of kids will share out, many learn to mentally disengage from the work at hand, knowing it doesn't matter if they generate ideas or not. An effective strategy to address this is to ask students to turn and share their thinking with a partner before bringing ideas to the whole group. Often referred to as pair-and-share or turn-and-talk, the simple act of prompting kids to *consistently* share their thinking with a neighbor is incredibly effective in building greater classroom engagement. This simple classroom structure:

- positions each of our students as someone who will have something to share
- provides every student an immediate outlet for their thinking
- offers those who are less confident an opportunity to access someone else's ideas before sharing out
- provides a degree of accountability.

What does it usually look like when we are listening closely?

- Looks at the speaker (eye contact) while they are speaking or at least checks in with their eyes from time-to-time
- Has a quiet mouth (whispering, singing, humming)
- Controlled body (might need to move/wiggle but not so much that it distracts others)

Figure 6.12
Students Name What Active
Listening Might Look Like

Figure 6.13
Students Show
They're Listening Closely

As such, having our students turn and talk on a regular basis promotes a more productive and democratic discussion where all students are supported to more fully participate.

Scaffolding Students to Build onto the Ideas of Others

We exert so much effort into making sure our students are actively listening during discussions because careful listening allows them to learn from others while at the same time positioning them to build onto the ideas of others in meaningful ways. The careful listening the kids engaged in during the discussion of water consumption enabled the class to create new understandings of hydration. In the following vignette my students engage in similar meaning making as they offer hypotheses in hopes of understanding why Black crime seems to be overreported on the news. Although at the beginning of the year I might have expected to hear children taking turns directing independent responses to me in hopes of "getting it right," in this discussion my participation is minimal. Elena, Peter, Caitlin, Kumail, and Laila speak directly to one another, trying to explain the unjust reporting Briana has noticed when watching the news (see Figure 6.14).

Briana 3-22
Why do People think mostly all black People are bad and not white People.

Figure 6.14
Briana's Entry in the Culture Journal

Briana: My question was, Why do people say mostly all Black people are bad and not that much white people?

Elena: No one thinks that.

Peter: Yeah, no one thinks that.

Chris: So why did you choose to put this question in the journal? What made you wonder about this?

Briana: Because when I see a lot of news, I see things saying about how a bunch of Black people are doing bad things but I don't see a lot of white people talked about. I know a lot of white people do bad things too, but I rarely ever see any of them have the word *bad*.

Peter: Well, some people would just judge people by how they look.

Elena: I think Black people never got a good start.

Chris: What do you mean by that?

Elena: 'Cause Black people had to do work picking fruits and vegetables and cotton and were poor at the beginning. White people stayed inside and had a break like sitting on the couch.

Chris: It's true lots of money was made on the backs of Black slaves who were not paid and were denied their freedom. I don't know that the white plantation owners sat inside on their couches all day.

Caitlin: I just learned this from a book. You know how Black people used to not be able to do things—like they had to sit in the back and in the balcony? Martin Luther King changed that. But some people still believe they should sit there.

Elena: That's what I mean by a bad start.

Kumail: That was mostly in America. Because in different countries there are Black people and I haven't seen that happen in those places.

Caitlin: Why are people here different?

Laila: Yeah. Why are so much Black people on the news but not so much white people? Does that mean people just don't want to put the white people on the news?

Kumail: Maybe because the newspeople are white or the people who own the news stations are white. Maybe that's what makes them think of that. Maybe they think they can do this because they're in charge.

Chris: I wonder if they even realize they're doing it. If Briana notices it, shouldn't they be able to notice it also? I wonder if there's someone we could talk to about this.

When we help our kids begin to speak *with* one another, we create conditions where they truly begin to explore complex topics. We can help them get here in three ways:

- resisting the urge to dominate the discussion
- offering stems that promote connections to others' thinking
- selectively calling on those poised to make a connection.

Resist the urge to dominate the discussion

As discussed earlier, a key part of accomplishing this is to resist the desire to respond to every child or to feel as though our perspective and knowledge desperately need to be heard in every instance. The benefit of our restraint is that it prompts students to fill these spaces with their own responses while conveying the message this really is *their* discussion.

Offer stems that promote connections to others' thinking

Another strategy to scaffold students into constructing collaborative discussions is to engage in a bit of teacher research and spend a few days recording all the different stems we hear students using when they successfully build onto each other's responses. When I listen to my own students and record their speech patterns in my teaching journal, I often capture phrases straight from their mouths, such as "Yeah, that's like . . . ," "Connecting to . . . ," "I agree with [insert name] because . . . ," and "I don't think that's right because. . . ." When we collect the natural language our students use and formally present it back to the class, we not only give value to those bridging their thinking to the contributions of others but also offer concrete models for those who aren't yet doing this work.

Selectively call on those who want to make connections

Lastly, another strategy to promote collaborative discussion is to briefly privilege the contributions of those who want to make connections or speak directly back to something that has already been shared. To do this, we ask our students to show us they intend to build onto someone else's idea by offering a visual cue—for instance, linking their two index fingers together—so we can call on them. Although not a strategy we would want to continue throughout the entire year, this physical prompt allows everyone in the circle to hear what it sounds like to have a discussion where people are working in *community with one another* rather than merely working in the presence of others. In their desire to participate in the discussion students will work deliberately to connect their thinking to that of their peers. However, it's important to note this is a strategy best used in small doses because, for all its best intentions, it tends to be a bit coercive and can result in wooden discussions where the need to make a connection (that is, to meet the teacher's demands) supersedes efforts to respond more naturally.

Learning to Value the Role of Disagreement in Exploratory Discussions

The final piece to helping our students elevate the quality of discussion is to teach the value of conflict (i.e., competing perspectives) in better understanding a given issue, better understanding ourselves, and better understanding those around us. Of course, competing perspectives often lead to disagreements. The tensions that grow from these differences in perspective can serve as a significant barrier for some students unless they're taught to value opportunities to hear from others who may see or experience the world differently. Without our support, such tensions can result in silence as many students fear being publicly doubted, questioned, or debated. Such experiences have the potential to challenge a student's social standing, position them as lacking knowledge, or cause them to fear offending others when speaking from the limitations of their own experiences and knowledge. Often, these are the very same reasons many teachers avoid discussions around sensitive topics. Therefore, we must teach our students to embrace disagreement as a necessity to more fully understanding an issue or topic—whether these differences in perspective ultimately cause them to change their minds or not.

The process of promoting open dialogue begins with creating a classroom that not only ensures students feel accepted and supported but also explicitly values the *process* of learning just as much as (if not more than) the *product* of learning. For instance, in our classroom knowing something is given no more attention or praise than working to figure something out. This helps students understand that what is valued is not an evaluation of who knows what or how much but rather who is actively engaged in pushing themselves to always learn more.

In the following vignette, we are just a few weeks into our second-grade school year and I'm working to accomplish three goals:

- position disagreements as a natural part of discussion
- introduce the belief that disagreements are a valuable part of learning
- model how we can speak to others in a respectful manner when challenging their beliefs.

To help my students put these principles into action, I selected a news article I felt would invite debate. The article spoke to the gendered nature of Halloween costumes, focusing on a mother who expressed disappointment in a national chain for offering boys many career-oriented Halloween costumes but offering only three such choices for her young daughter.

Chris: So, I've been thinking about how sometimes when you go to a pizza restaurant not everyone in your family necessarily agrees on the best pizza to order for the family. Right? Some people might want pepperoni. Others might want cheese or barbecue chicken. Sometimes these sorts of disagreements can lead to arguments—or even hurt feelings. Hopefully not, but maybe.

(*Various voices erupt to respond to this.*)

Chris: We also sometimes disagree about movies or TV shows or music or books. We disagree about what to play at recess. We disagree about all sorts of things. It's natural. We're different people who see things in our own way and sometimes we want very different things.

But I'm especially interested in how these differences of opinion emerge when we have discussions about what's right and what's wrong. We hear people say, "You need to do the right thing." But what *is* right? *Who* gets to decide that? *How* do they decide? What if others disagree?

This article I just read you is like that. We're getting ready to discuss what you're thinking about the costume choices, the mother, the store, and the little girl. I'm really interested to hear what you have to say about all this. I predict we may not all see it exactly the same way. But I bet our disagreements might help us understand the article a little bit better because we'll be pushed to think about it differently than maybe we did at first on our own. So, listen closely to what others have to say and ask yourself how you feel about what you hear. Do you agree? Do you disagree? I want to know what you're thinking.

So, who'd like to start us off? What were you thinking about the article, Martin?

Martin: I think the girl in the article should just choose one of the three costumes at the store and then hope she gets lucky next year. Maybe they'll have more.

Chris: So Martin is saying it's OK that she only had three choices. She could just choose one of the three and hope that next year she'll have more options to select from. Who wants to respond to Martin? You're either going to respond to him by agreeing or you can respond by disagreeing. Just be sure to speak respectfully and really explain your thinking so we can understand how you arrived at your opinion.

Noah: I sort of disagree that there needs to be more choices because my mom doesn't work. She only subs for classes at the gym. I think that's why girls have so few career costumes. It's because the dads work and the girls rarely work—but they sometimes work.

Elena: My mom works at a very hard job!

Alex: My mom works too.

Peter: Yeah, I know. My mom works at the university.

Chris: So, some people are disagreeing with Noah about his idea that dads work more than moms.

Peter: I don't think that's true.

Chris: Noah, you're saying that in your family's experience your mom's work is less regular than your dad's work?

Noah: Yeah.

Chris: OK. I don't necessarily think that's the truth in all our homes, though. Certainly it's not true in mine. There were a number of years, when my children were babies, that my wife worked as a teacher and I worked at home to take care of our kids. My wife's work was in the classroom and my work was at home caring for our children. Working parents can look different from one family to the next. Certainly we see that here in our classroom with our families. It's good to share out what we're noticing and what we're thinking so others can add to our ideas and maybe even push us to see things differently. For instance, you might be interested to learn more about all the jobs our mothers have in this classroom. I'm not sure you know about all the careers our mothers have.

Presenting access to competing views on a particular issue is critical to meaning making in that it offers students an opportunity to both consider and critique a wealth of perspectives. In this small piece of discussion, Noah's perspective that men's careers are more serious provided others in the classroom an opportunity to hear a worldview that directly contradicted their own experiences as children of working mothers employed in a wide variety of jobs and careers. Hearing this, these students were able to practice speaking back to ideas they knew to be untrue as well as to hear how an adult deals respectfully but directly with untrue claims.

Furthermore, by allowing Noah to share his developing thoughts, I was able to address this untruth. To have avoided conflict in our discussions would have meant, in this case, allowing Noah's thoughts on female employment to remain and perhaps even grow. This is what happens when blind logic, based on little to no firsthand knowledge, goes unchecked. Too often we see adults actively avoid firsthand knowledge (such as the experiences of immigrants who've come here illegally) for fear this will challenge what they've already invested years in believing. More often than not, people do not like to have their beliefs challenged. But they should. Over the course of a school year (or more hopefully, well beyond) students should be given numerous opportunities to engage in contested discussions as they continually refine their understandings of the world around them and learn to push back against beliefs they find harmful to themselves or to others within their communities.

Watch ▶

Using Metaphor and Restatement with Kindergartners: Notice how Tiffany uses a physical metaphor to help kindergartners understand justice. She recognizes how important it is for each child to be able to put these complex thoughts into their own words, thus making them their own.

A Science Journal Entry Leads to Discussion of Ways of Knowing: A student asks, "Can birds read?" The class hypothesizes based on what they know, and wonder about what other information might be needed.

Examples of Short Classroom Journal Shares: Not all classroom journal sharing in Morning Meeting turns into a longer discussion. Here are some examples of shorter shares.

Morning Meeting Discussion Strategies: In this clip, Chris focuses on Morning Meeting discussion strategies and helps his students grow more comfortable with disagreements within a discussion while also demonstrating our understanding of issues is tentative and evolving.

Supporting
Students to
Speak Up

7

Chris: Does anyone else have a journal this morning?

Elena: I do. I wrote a question in the Classroom Community Journal. I was wondering why some people don't talk very much at Morning Meeting.

Chris: Ah, that's an interesting question. I'm curious to hear what people have to say. But you know what, I think we should ask those who don't feel like they share all that often to be the ones who explain this to us. They're best prepared to help us understand it since they're the ones who actually experience it. You know what I mean? Others who talk a lot would just be guessing. We should go straight to the source. So, does anyone want to start us off? Maybe someone who doesn't feel like they share all that often?

Elena: [*Looking to see who raises their hands*] Emi.

Emi: I don't know why people are sometimes not talking. I know I don't talk very much but I'm trying to work on it. I just don't really like talking that much. I'm usually very quiet. So, I don't really talk that much.

Elena: Jolina.

Jolina: Well, I'm one of the people who don't really talk a lot so I have the experience too. I don't talk a lot because I don't really have answers to lots of things.

Alex: But you can just give an idea. That's what I do.

Jolina: But people ask about things I don't really know the answer to. Or I don't have a thought to that question.

Alex: Oh.

Chris: This makes me think one thing we could do to is to make sure we give everyone enough time to think about these questions before people share out. Some of us, like me, often need more time to think about things before we're ready to go public with our thoughts. It takes us a bit more time to carefully think through everything. Maybe if we had more time to think, we'd feel more comfortable sharing out.

Elena: Anyone else?

Noah: Well, I talk a lot sometimes but sometimes I'm quiet too. It's like we talked about yesterday, sometimes I just don't feel comfortable with the topic because—like if it's about gender or something—I'm afraid I might say something that will hurt someone's feelings.

Engaging in classroom discussions poses a substantial challenge for many of our students. Whether it's their shyness, need for longer think time, or inability to get in a word edgewise, these students often find themselves on the outside of whole-group efforts to explore new ideas. I've found this to be especially true when classroom discussions turn to sensitive issues. These discussions present a whole new set of challenges for our students—ones they don't face when merely sharing math strategies or analyzing the relationship between character and plot. This is because the thoughts shared during critical discussions are often personal. With so many diverse experiences, understandings, and perspectives at play, the ideas that emerge have the potential to lead to hurt feelings, guilt, and even strained relationships. With time, this potential for harm can negatively affect our kids' willingness to participate for fear they might say something wrong.

It's this tinge of discomfort that leads many teachers to delicately tiptoe through conversations related to difference—ever careful to avoid introducing or exploring injustice and oppression. This desire to play it safe fosters color blindness. In place of critical thought and honest reflection, teachers (namely those from dominant social groups) too often adopt the "We're all the same" mantra. Although this belief holds some bit of truth, it blatantly ignores not only the presence of our differences but also the many ways the dominant culture works to exploit them. As bell hooks (1994) argues, avoiding discussions of systemic social injustices to protect our students from discomfort is wrong. Our classrooms should not always be a safe, harmonious place. If our "safe" classroom is one that chooses to protect the feelings of those from dominant social groups while allowing oppressive beliefs and practices to remain unchecked, we must ask ourselves "Who is it exactly I'm keeping 'safe'?" and conversely, "Who, through my silence, am I allowing to be harmed?"

The discomfort our kids sometimes experience during these discussions is necessary but need not be permanent—and certainly not stifling. We can coach them through these feelings. In truth, one of the most generative things we can hope to achieve with our students is to help them learn to productively discuss important topics in diverse settings. Given the toxic state of public discourse around issues of difference in our nation today, we'd do well to invest in such a goal for future generations.

In this chapter I will share some of the most significant challenges our students face when presented with opportunities to discuss sensitive topics in the classroom. These include:

- a perceived lack of knowledge

- a fear of upsetting others

- a discomfort with hearing hard truths

- a lack of trust in the teacher and/or their classmates.

Perceived Lack of Knowledge: "I don't have a thought to that question."

One obstacle many of our kids face is the fact they've never truly considered these types of issues before. They're not yet sure what to make of these issues or how to respond (Figure 7.1). This is especially true of our white students. Families from privileged social groups aren't often compelled to discuss the presence of social injustices with their children. Likely, they fail to see the point in it, harking back to the problematic nature of the good/bad binary, because white parents don't see themselves as racist or as holding any learned biases. They don't feel it's necessary to do any work to address these issues. It's enough for them to simply raise children who are "kind."

Key Components of Justice-Oriented Discussions

Elena: I wrote a question in the Classroom Community Journal. I was wondering why some people don't talk very much at Morning Meeting.

Chris: Ah, that's an interesting question. I'm curious to hear what people have to say. But you know what, I think we should ask those who don't feel like they share all that often to be the ones who explain this to us. They're best prepared to help us understand it since they're the ones who actually experience it. You know what I mean? Others who talk a lot would just be guessing. We should go straight to the source. So, does anyone want to start us off? Maybe someone who doesn't feel like they share all that often? ← Explicitly Naming Just Practices

Elena: [*Looking to see who raises their hands*] Emi. ← Student-Led Discussion

Emi: I don't know why people are sometimes not talking. I know I don't talk very much but I'm trying to work on it. I just don't really like talking that much. I'm usually very quiet. So, I don't really talk that much. ← Self-Reflection

Explicitly Naming Just Practices: Although it's important to privilege voices in the class who have firsthand knowledge of a subject, it is also important that we explicitly name what we are doing when deferring to these voices. Doing so allows our students to learn the value of going straight to the source rather than relying on the blind logic of others.

Student-Led Discussion: Once students pose a question in Morning Meeting, they should be put in charge of that discussion. This takes the form of calling on classmates who are interested in responding. Another option with great potential is to offer them the final word. In taking the final word, they restate their question and then tell us what they're thinking after having talked it through with others in the circle. By putting our students in charge of these discussions, we support them into greater agency in hopes they'll launch similar discussions outside of the classroom.

Self-Reflection: Self-reflection is a critical part of the social justice classroom. Here, Emi reflects on why she rarely shares out during class discussions. Reflecting on this prepares her to begin the process of addressing it. It also helps others understand her better and, when possible, extend the support she needs.

Figure 7.1

Key Components of Justice-Oriented Discussions

When I ask my kids to talk about how critical discussions take place at home with their families, many of the responses I receive from white students tend to follow this pattern.

Colton: We don't really talk about it.

Peter: Yeah, we don't either.

Chris: So you don't talk about it at all?

Colton: My mom and dad say to be nice to other people and not to be mean.

Chris: Well, that's part of it for sure. Do you ever talk about how some groups of people are treated unfairly and what you can do to stop this?

Colton: No.

Chris: Has anyone ever suggested to you the fact we all sometimes believe hurtful things about groups of people unlike ourselves but maybe we don't even notice we're doing it?

Colton: Uh-uh.

But not only white students struggle with these discussions. We can't assume our minoritized students have had much experience with them either. Some have, but certainly not all. And even for those who have, these discussions have likely been focused on just one or two particular issues (say, racism) while completely ignoring others (homophobia, sexism, xenophobia, nationalism, etc.). For this reason we shouldn't be surprised when our students confess, as Jolina did, "I don't have a thought to that question."

So, what can we do to support our kids to overcome their reluctance?

Provide Our Students the Background Knowledge They Require

First, we need to provide students the background knowledge necessary to make sense of these issues. This comes in the form of shared news articles, videos, stories, and trade books. As detailed in Chapter 5, when we carefully select texts depicting a wide variety of characters, issues, and historical accounts, we offer students an opportunity to draw upon the stories and ideas of others when formulating the thoughts they'd like to share with the class.

Prompt Our Students to Share What They're Thinking or Wondering About

Second, we can gently fold them into our discussions with carefully worded invitations. An important component of this is the assumption they have something to add. When we publicly assume our kids *would* know or have an idea about the topic at hand (i.e., "Jolina, tell me what you're thinking or wondering about all of this"), we help them begin to see themselves in the same way (Johnston 2004). Such invitations not only position our kids as people with something to share but also provide them an entry point into the discussion. This is especially helpful for those who aren't yet brave enough to lift their hand into the air. As with anything else we teach, we can provide them the support and encouragement they need to grow more confidence in themselves.

Fear of Upsetting Others: "I was afraid I might say the wrong thing."

Students often fear saying something that might hurt others or be perceived as offensive or hurtful. One day I pulled a group of boys aside to follow up on a recent class discussion we'd had about gender inequity. During the whole-group discussion I'd noticed some of the boys who generally spoke quite often seemed to remain uncharacteristically quiet. I asked them if anything had caused them to curb their participation.

> **Peter:** Yeah, I was worried because I was afraid I might say the wrong thing because one time, I don't mean no offense, Colton, but—
>
> **Colton:** No offense, bro.
>
> **Peter:** —one time Colton accidentally said the wrong thing and everyone was like "Colton!"
>
> **Colton:** Yeah! Like every time when the boys say something wrong the girls are like "Aah!"
>
> **Noah:** Yeah, that happened to me too and I felt bad because I wasn't trying to hurt anyone's feelings or make them mad.

Sure enough, they were right. There *had* been times the kids (regardless of gender) openly and assertively shared their frustration with a classmate for having said something they found offensive. Noah's experience with this had an especially lasting impact. Months earlier, during a discussion detailed in Chapter 6 about the fact girls have so few items to choose from when searching for a career-oriented Halloween costume, he'd used the employment status of his own parents as a source of knowledge in trying to explain why girls may have so few choices in costumes.

> **Noah:** I sort of disagree that there needs to be more choices because my mom doesn't work. She only subs for classes at the gym. I think that's why girls have so few career costumes. It's because the dads work and the girls rarely work—but they sometimes work.
>
> **Elena:** My mom works a very hard job!
>
> **Alex:** My mom works too.
>
> **Peter:** Yeah, I know. My mom works at the university.

The retorts from his friends were immediate and filled with both resentment and indignation. Though we were trying to learn to respectfully disagree, there had been an obvious spike in emotions around the room. Noah, an incredibly kind and respectful child who worked hard each day to care for his peers, instantly retreated into his shell. He hadn't considered the fact his perspective might offend others. After he'd brought this up again during my chat with the boys, I asked him if this experience had stopped him from sharing his thoughts at other times during the year.

> **Noah:** Yeah, because I don't want to say the wrong thing or I don't want to offend someone and they're going to get mad. I don't want to hurt someone's feelings. And it's like I would be really uncomfortable if I did say something wrong and I don't want to do that again. In a few discussions I knew I'd say something that probably would offend someone so I decided not to say it. So I felt uncomfortable.

Noah's concerns for being open with the group are understandable. So were the other group members' frustrations with hearing something they felt belittled the important work their mothers did. Yet, if the classroom environment forces students like Noah to conceal his faulty thinking, how can we expect to help him and so many others to move beyond their current beliefs? When students feel silenced, not only do we lose out on teachable moments but we also run the risk of allowing feelings of resentment to eventually fester and grow. Charles Blow (2018) refers to the result as "back-against-the-wall, no-more-space-to-retreat moment[s] of fighting back, of pushing back, of standing proud in their patriarchy and proclaiming it will not bend." Silencing these voices does not further the cause of social justice. It undermines it.

That said, words hurt and the potential for harm goes both ways. For this reason, we cannot establish conditions that work to protect the speaker without ensuring we're protecting the listener as well. Although we want open and honest dialogue, we certainly cannot allow these discussions to become a free-for-all where one's freedom of speech and right to grow and learn from one's errors in thought override the rights of others to feel protected from the underlying messages being communicated within oppressive beliefs. We must walk this line carefully.

To build an environment that promotes open discussion that is both healthy and respectful, we can:

- help our students see growth and understanding as one of our primary goals
- model how one might respond to something they find offensive.

Help Our Students See Growth and Understanding as One of Our Primary Goals

It's important that we help our students recognize the fact we're all working to better understand the complexities of race, gender, religion, gender identity, and so on, and that this process can sometimes be messy. Our growth relies on others' willingness to hear our current thinking—especially when that thinking is in serious need of revision. But to navigate these situations (such as when Noah felt attacked for not knowing so many mothers had careers), we need to first help our kids learn how to respond to ideas they find offensive in ways that are more likely to convince others to engage in self-reflection and critique. For instance, we might begin:

Chris: One thing I've noticed in our discussions is that sometimes people say something that might make a lot of sense to them in the moment but when others hear this idea they don't like it at all. In fact, they're offended by it. They feel like the idea is not only wrong but hurtful. I'll give you an example.

Imagine our class having a discussion about why girls aren't allowed to play football in some youth football leagues. Some might say girls don't really like football all that much so it doesn't really matter. Others might say they'd love to play football and it's wrong they're not allowed to. Others, still, might say most girls aren't interested in football right now but should definitely have the right to try it if they want to. And maybe, in the middle of all of this, I might think it over and say, "Well, I think they're not allowed to because they're not tough enough to play youth football."

Now, I'm not saying I agree with this statement at all. In fact, I don't. But I'm putting it out there as an example of the sort of thing that might cause some people in the room to feel angry, disrespected, or even hurt. In fact, I noticed by the change in body language just now that some people did in fact feel angered by it. But here's the thing: If someone believed this was true and we strongly disagreed with them, how should we respond? Or maybe a better question is, what is it we hope to accomplish when we speak back to them?

Our kids must come to see the power and potential of helping others more closely question and critique their own thinking. This is not likely to happen under the threat of being judged or attacked. To the contrary, those who feel judged or attacked are more likely to dig in all the deeper. Just as we all assume different timelines as developing readers, writers, and mathematicians, we must afford one another the same grace when it comes to more clearly seeing others for the beauty and power of who they are.

Model How One Might Respond to Something They Find Offensive

Another key piece is to treat an incident when someone shares something offensive as a teachable moment. In doing so, we demonstrate how one might respond in such situations. Although it's true we want to position our kids as primary meaning makers within these discussions, I can't stress enough the fact it's *our* role to ensure all forms of misinformation be problematized and debunked, especially when they communicate harmful beliefs about any group of people. Recognizing the fact our kids have diverse experiences and worldviews does not mean we're required to humor or even consider oppressive perspectives. Yet, we *can* show our students a more productive path to dealing with these tricky situations. When I do this in the classroom I try to address these statements in three parts: (1) I first challenge the validity of the statement, (2) then I explain that such misinformation or views work to oppress groups of people, and (3) I conclude by providing contrasting information or perspectives.

For example, one morning during the campaign season leading up to the 2016 election Malik started Morning Meeting by asking, "So some of you might think that Donald Trump isn't but my question is, why do people say Donald Trump is racist?" Immediately, the discussion turned to the proposed border wall as a response to people entering from Mexico.

Malik: My Nana told me that and my family thinks it. Why I think it too is because he wants to build a wall around the United States so people from other countries can't walk in from Mexico.

Colton: My mom told me about that.

Malik: I'm wondering why he would do the wall.

Kumail: Because Mexicans like to get into America.

Caitlin: They're just trying to get away from their horrible life, and they don't want to have to do a lot of work and pay money to get in. So they sneak in to get away from Mexico because they don't like their property. They don't like their place. In Mexico there's a hard life and they want to get away from it.

Chris: So I'd like to stop for a moment and think more about some of the ideas being shared right now because they're not all exactly true. In fact, I think some of these ideas are not only false but they could be *dangerous* because they play into negative stereotypes. Just like there are stereotypes about girls or people from the South or Black people, there are also stereotypes about people in Mexico. And stereotypes hurt people. This is why we have to be careful not to fall into the trap of believing them. So I'm really glad these came out just now because we get a chance to think about them a little more closely.

I was able to speak directly to the fact false information was being shared and that such misinformation can negatively impact people's lives. Yet it's important to note there was no anger in my voice. There was no negative body language or pained facial expressions. I was matter-of-fact. This clinical approach might be a challenge for some teachers when confronted with such words. To be honest, there are many times when it's a challenge for me. Caitlin's assessment of Mexicans as people who "don't want to have to do a lot of work" was incredibly offensive. Yet her miscue was not coming from any type of hatred but rather her own ignorance. This is why I refer to it as a "miscue." Caitlin had blindly accepted this belief, as children do, when hearing it somewhere along the way from trusted adults. We each carry our own fair share of cultural ignorance, so we should all be able to relate. When we begin to see ourselves as a work in progress prone to making false assumptions of our own about others, it becomes easier to do the same with our students. Knowing such a statement cannot go unchallenged for fear of becoming accepted fact for all the others in the classroom, I wanted in this moment to show my kids how we can respond to oppressive beliefs in a way that invites people to more closely consider those things they wrongly assume to be true.

Chris: The fact of the matter is there are very wealthy people who live in Mexico. However, not everyone there is wealthy. Not even close, kind of like here in America. Many Mexicans, like many Americans, can work really, really hard and still not have the opportunity to get their families everything they need. It's a challenge many countries face. But just because some people are poor doesn't mean they don't work hard.

In many cases they work even harder because they have longer hours or work multiple jobs in hopes of making enough money to support their families. For lots of people in Mexico, they see more opportunity in America—more jobs and better pay. So they come here. Sometimes they come legally and other times they feel their only hope is to sneak in illegally. This is where our national debate begins: What should we do when faced with the problem of people coming here illegally but also knowing how badly they need these jobs and the money for their family? Finding a solution everyone agrees with has been a challenge. What do you think, Caitlin? What could we do?

When I have felt less sure about how to speak back to a student's miscue, I've often fallen back on statements such as "I'm not sure that sounds right to me but I'd like for us to investigate it further." Such a response ensures harmful statements do not go unchallenged while also inviting further inquiry and discussion. However, in the preceding vignette I knew precisely how I wanted to navigate Caitlin's miscue. After sharing information that contradicted her initial statements, I carefully folded her right back into the discussion to ensure she didn't feel shut down by me or anyone else. This is a critical move and one that warrants careful thought (see Figure 7.2). We wanted to hear Caitlin's voice. We needed her to be part of our efforts to create

Tool

Knowing our students often fear how their peers may respond to a given idea, it shouldn't be surprising to learn they also fear what their teachers will have to say. In fact, a teacher's words can be even more impactful given they possess such power within the classroom. To make certain we respond to miscues in a manner that promotes continued participation and reflection, we must be deliberate in our approach. Here are some options:	
Framing the miscue as a valuable opportunity	"I'm really glad these [ideas] came out just now because we get to think about them a little more closely."
Sharing our own history of miscues	"I can think of a time when I mistakenly believed something kind of similar to that."
Shifting blame to the social forces at play	"I can imagine you must have heard, somewhere, that was true. I sometimes hear the same things."
Inviting them to immediately jump back in	"So, what do you think?"

Figure 7.2
How to Gently Fold Kids Back In After They've Miscued

meaning. Our goal in these discussions is never to make children agree with our positions on such matters. That said, we do expect them to gain richer insight into the lives of others so that when they make their own determinations, they're built upon a broader and more accurate body of knowledge. Our stances should not be based on stereotypes or misinformation.

Discomfort with Hearing Hard Truths: "It's kind of scary."

To this point the kids' responses have focused on the struggles they face as speakers in these discussions. However, another pattern I've noticed is when children feel some tension after learning about the hurtful beliefs present within their communities—beliefs they hadn't even known existed. For instance, one morning I asked a group of girls to reflect on our class discussions related to gender. I asked, "Has there been anything about these discussions that's made you feel uncomfortable or caused you worry?"

Jolina: I think I feel a little disturbed sometimes because some people think girls are weaker than males.

Caitlin: Yeah, I felt sort of bad hearing what the boys do. I didn't even know that happened.

Chris: So you were surprised to hear people did things like keep girls from going to college or that it was harder for women to get into positions of power at some jobs?

Elena: Yeah. It's kind of scary. Like, what's going to happen? You don't know about it and then you hear and you're like "Aah!" Girls get it so bad and you're like, "Is this going to happen to you or something?"

Chris: You mean like the costumes? Or like the women's national soccer team getting paid less?

Jolina: Yeah, and we didn't even know.

Elena: Yeah, because you never thought of it. You never even knew of it and now you're just like "Hey, that's just like unfair!"

By this point in their young lives they already had numerous experiences where they were told what girls should play with and how girls should dress. They'd watched other people laugh at boys when they lost to a girl and they'd been excluded at times from certain games on the recess field for allegedly "not being good enough." All of these things frustrated them and they were ready to push back. Yet, it wasn't until our discussions that they started to realize this was bigger than just a few boys they knew. As they and their classmates began to watch the world a little more closely and ask questions about what they saw, they suddenly noticed troubling patterns. They saw it in the way the toy aisles were arranged at the store. They saw it in the ways girls were being depicted in media. They saw it when learning about pay gaps and underrepresentation in executive offices. They saw it everywhere . . . and they didn't like it.

They weren't alone. Other students shared similar moments when they were shocked to find out the world was less fair than they'd once believed. And even those who already knew these oppressions existed (namely, students of Color and those who practiced non-Christian religions) were disappointed at times to hear a classmate reveal they'd accepted such beliefs without really questioning their validity or meaning and how it affected their friends. This was most evident one day when Colton suggested, by pounding his fist into his open hand, that he'd have a hard time accepting anyone who didn't believe in a Christian God. His very best friend, Kumail, sat three spots down, looking at him in puzzlement as he wondered if this meant him, since his family was Hindu and he had openly shared aspects of his faith with the class on previous occasions.

There's an old cliché, "Ignorance is bliss." But is it? Do we want to continue walking through an unjust world blind not only to the oppressions faced by others but also to our own role in perpetuating the conditions under which they operate? I know my students don't. I often ask them at the end of the year as we reflect back on all we've explored, "Knowing how hard these discussions can be at times, do you think kids should talk about this stuff at school?" Despite the occasional discomfort they've experienced, almost all tell me they still think it's worth it. After sharing the fact there were times they felt some concern for what this all meant for their futures, Caitlin, Elena, and Malia concluded:

Caitlin: Well, I think classes should talk about this stuff so they can change.

Elena: And so we just know. So we just know and we can know how to do it.

Malia: Yeah, and we can fix it. And keep it changed.

So, how do we navigate this? How do we continue the important work but at the same time ensure that our kids are not overwhelmed? Two practices that I've found helpful are to:

- Allow our students space to decompress and breathe.
- Carefully determine what is appropriate and what is not.

Allow Our Students Space to Decompress and Breathe

A friend recently shared a story with me about an experience her ten-year-old son had when visiting his grandparents. During his visit a discussion of Trump's immigration policy came up and his grandfather told him, "Don't worry, they're only going to send the bad people home." Her son was deeply affected by hearing this come from his grandfather and called home to talk about it. He soon began to cry as he explained to his mother why he was bothered by his grandfather's belief those being deported were "bad people." His mother assured him they'd work together to help those families facing deportation once he returned home. To prepare, she conducted research and generated a list of things they could do to address this together. Yet when he returned home a few days later, he didn't want to deal with it any longer. It was too much. He felt he just needed to leave it alone for a while.

The weight of these issues and our feelings around them can be a lot to process. For this reason, we need to be careful to make sure inquiries into injustice are consistent while at the same time balanced within many other aspects of our social justice work. That is to say, a little social critique goes a long way. When not tackling issues of oppressive thought and action, we can still be actively affirming our students' identities on a regular basis through rich stories, inclusive histories, and invitations to share important pieces of their home lives with us. These are wondrous celebrations of self and the world we live in. This work around identity and diversity helps each of us feel better prepared and more fully refreshed for the depth of our inquiries into injustice and the hateful beliefs that underpin them.

Carefully Determine What Is Appropriate and What Is Not

We must also be deliberate when deciding what's appropriate and what's not, given the specifics of our classrooms. If we want to make certain our kids are not overwhelmed by this work, we need to make informed choices as to what topics are most appropriate for their age, maturity, and life experiences.

For instance, although I explore how differences are used to justify the mistreatment of people, I tread very lightly when addressing other aspects of this, such as hate crimes. Acts of extreme violence present a real dilemma. Some choose the easy path, which is to ignore this reality. Yet what happens when these stories become national headlines and a number of our kids overhear bits and pieces on the evening news or on the car ride to school? To expect our children to process this frightening and confusing information on their own without the guidance and care of a trusted adult seems immoral, if not dangerous.

But at the same time when we do choose to discuss these stories, we must be careful in our approach. Elementary-aged children don't need to know about body counts or the traumatizing experiences of those who've been targeted. This sort of information is far too graphic. What they *do* need is to understand we all have a role to play in disrupting ignorance and hate. And above all, while they need to understand oppressive beliefs and practices play a role in such acts, they also need to understand they are safe and well cared for.

One other piece of this work is to heavily scrutinize the value of engagements intended to coerce children into empathy. For a short time before securing my first teaching job, I served as a substitute teacher. One day when working in a third-grade classroom, I was told we would be conducting a simulation of the Trail of Tears. At precisely 9:30 that morning each of the third-grade teachers began yelling at their eight- and nine-year-old children to quickly gather all their belongs and get out the door. At first, students began laughing. They assumed it was some sort of joke. However, after repeated demands they were finally convinced this was no joke. They were given mere seconds to get their things collected and get moving. These children were marched through the halls as their teachers tore into them relentlessly for dropping folders and pencils while at the same time demanding they walk faster or else suffer unnamed consequences. It was an unsettling sight to behold. Some students were in tears, most were frightened, and all were in some amount of shock. Though there was a debriefing session at the end to put all this into some sort of twisted context, the ends fell far short of the means. Personally, I chose not to actively participate in this simulation. That said, I most certainly *did* participate. I participated by not speaking up, not taking action to stop it. Looking back, it's one of my greatest regrets in teaching.

Experiences like these take place in schools across the country far too often. If it's not a misguided simulation, it's instances where teachers choose to present videos or photos that are meant to enlighten children but are far more likely to demoralize or traumatize them. One example among many is the presentation of photographs depicting children being physically removed from their parents and kept in cages as part of Donald Trump's crackdown on immigration. What fear such photos must create in the hearts of young children—particularly those who've been removed from their own families due to circumstances out of their control. Discussions of immigration need not include mental images that have the potential to haunt our students' dreams. There are far more just methodologies, such as those presented in this book.

Lack of Trust in the Teacher: "I don't want to go there with her."

In his book *Not Light, But Fire* Matthew Kay (2018) writes about a time a student entered his classroom upset by a discussion in her previous class. The discussion had been intended to address protests in Ferguson, Missouri, in response to the fatal shooting of Michael Brown, an eighteen-year-old Black man, by a white police officer. The student was angered by negative comments made about the Black protestors but even more upset by the fact these comments were left unchallenged by her white teacher. Hearing this, one of her classmates admitted, "I don't want to talk about Ferguson with white people. No matter how liberal they are, it's still going to be just . . . academic for them. But it's our actual lives. We really have to *be* Black when this stuff is going on. I don't have the energy to explain my emotions every time a teacher decides to talk about race."

We shouldn't be surprised to learn there are times students tread lightly into sensitive discussions with us—if they choose to tread at all. Yes, our social identities play a key role. When we cannot speak to social issues from personal experience, we are likely at times to be met with healthy doses of skepticism from those who truly do live these experiences, either directly or indirectly. Our motives are questioned and, as shared previously, some may feel overwhelmed by the continual effort that is required to *bring us along*.

This is not limited to race. There have undoubtedly been times in our own lives when the particulars of our identities have caused us to oversimplify, misrepresent, or fumble around a myriad of complex issues. For instance, most of us lack the personal experiences necessary to fully understand what it's like to be a Muslim living in post–9/11 America. Many of us also don't know how it feels to live under the constant fear of deportation. And a number of us have never been forced to worry about where our next meal would come from or where we'd be sleeping next week. No matter who we are, there will always be times we lack the personal experience to fully understand the issue at hand. Despite the kindness in our hearts and the sincerity of our intentions there will be times when students are understandably unwilling to put themselves out there emotionally. They know all too well these discussions pose a danger to them as multiple perspectives fill the room.

To navigate this I suggest we first accept the fact we can invite children into these discussions but there are going to be times when our students have legitimate reasons to disengage. Although I don't consider having one's privilege challenged to be a worthy reason, I do have serious concern for children from marginalized communities because they are the ones who are most vulnerable. Understanding this, it's imperative we give these students the time and space they need while at the same time working to build trust within the classroom community—especially in discussions where we are positioned as part of the dominant culture. Trust is key. No matter who we are, what we believe, or what causes we've committed ourselves to in the present or the past, each new group of kids comes to us unsure of this all. It is our responsibility to understand their concerns and act accordingly.

Watch ▶

Second Graders Ethan and Kiersten Explain Classroom Journals: As Ethan explains, "If we didn't have classroom journals, where would we have to share our ideas?"

The Slow Process of Learning How to Listen to Each Other: Second- and third-grade teacher Chris shares developmental expectations.

Valuing Engagement Over Closure: Teacher Chris explains what his goals are in student discussion and how they help restrain the instinct to tell students what they should know.

When Talk Leads to Action

8

Once students learn to build discussions about those things they feel are unjust, it's critical we teach them to act on their convictions. Without action, there can be no change, and we risk children becoming cynical about our intentions. It took me some time to grow into this realization. For years I fell into the trap of merely teaching my students *about* social justice. I helped them identify and discuss the issues that concerned them but never really asked them to do much with this information. Looking back, I realize I should have expected so much more from them, as well as from myself. Let this be a cautionary tale to us both. We cannot spin our wheels teaching *about* social justice when what we really need to be doing is teaching *for* social justice. As so many young activists have demonstrated across the globe, from Marley Diaz's #1000blackgirlbooks campaign to Greta Thunberg's organization of climate strikes throughout the world, our students are never too young to begin making positive changes in their communities. Our role is to nudge them along, helping them develop the agency, knowledge, and skills they need to be successful (see Figure 8.1).

For social justice advocacy, students need . . .	What does this mean?	What does it look like?

Agency	To take action, our kids must first imagine themselves as someone capable of making a difference. They must recognize the potential they possess to shape future outcomes.	We consistently invite students to take an active stance and expect change by asking students, "It seems like [you/a lot of people] care about this issue. Are you interested in taking action? What actions might we take that will get at the root causes of this issue?"
		
		This may include:
		
		- Personal behavior changes now that we know better
		- Communication, such as
		  - Engaging in letter-writing campaigns to key decision makers
		  - Speaking at public forums
		  - Asking advocacy groups, "We believe in this cause and the work you're doing. How can we help?"

Contextual Knowledge	To ensure they're not working from partial or biased information as well as to help them make a stronger case for their cause, students increase their understanding of the issue through research.	We seek out opportunities to learn alongside one another. These inquires are framed by intentional questions that allow children to *learn how to learn*, such as:
		
		- "How can we learn more about the root causes of this issue?"
		  - "Who could we talk to/invite into the classroom who might know a lot about this?"
		  - "What sorts of texts could we collect to help us learn more?" Or "Who might be able to help us find some texts so we can learn more about this?"

For social justice advocacy, students need . . .	What does this mean?	What does it look like?
Explicit Connections Between School Learning and the Action in the Larger World	Students achieve a greater sense of purpose in their schooling when learning is connected to agentive action.	We ask, "How can we use the skills we're learning in school to advocate for this issue?" We integrate our social justice work into existing state standards that call on students to: • Write arguments that support our claims using relevant evidence and express those claims in a logical sequence. • Strategically use multiple modalities and multimedia to communicate ideas. • Draw conclusions from bar graphs, picture graphs, and object graphs. • Demonstrate the skills necessary to address shared problems in a respectful and productive manner.

Figure 8.1
Framework for Supporting Student Action

Last spring two of my students shared an article titled "Making Columbia a 'City of Women': Group advocates for representation on landmarks" (Ellis 2019). The article pointed to the fact there were numerous downtown streets named after men but only one, Lady Street, named in honor of a woman (Martha Washington). When the ensuing discussion began to wind down, I asked everyone how they felt about the fact there was so little representation of women on city street signs and landmarks. As I suspected, they felt this was wildly unfair. I then asked, "Is anyone interested in trying to do something to change this?" A few hands immediately shot into the air. Soon, many others joined them. This was the first step: helping my kids develop greater agency by imagining themselves as someone capable of working for change.

Over the months that followed, we welcomed a series of visitors into the classroom to help us better understand this issue. First, we met with the journalist who wrote the article. She was grateful her work had inspired young children to want to learn more. She shared some of her research notes with us—including the fact there were 145 street names and landmarks named for influential people across the entire city yet only 4 percent of these represented women. Next, we invited classroom families, school board members, local professors, district office personnel, and many others to come in and help us think more about this issue. Each person who visited was asked to teach us about one or two women whose life's work they found inspiring. Our goal was to uncover the stories that had long been overlooked and undervalued. Although this list encompassed women from around the globe, we later refined it to include just those from our home state. This was our second step: engaging in extended research to more fully understand the issue.

When we felt we had a fairly solid understanding, we invited the mayor into the classroom so we could present our concerns, research findings, and expectations. As he sat comfortably in a chair at the front of the classroom, the children meticulously laid out the issue, spoke to their concerns for how a lack of representation affects us all, provided a detailed summary of the inspiring women who deserved to be memorialized, and made a formal request to have this issue addressed. The mayor was moved by the depths of their passion and knowledge. He not only commended them for the work they were doing but asked if they'd be willing to address the full city council on this issue. A few months later they headed down to city hall to provide a formal presentation as well as give interviews to the local press (see Figure 8.2). As with the earlier presentation in our classroom, we carefully brainstormed what needed to be shared and how we thought we should go about sharing this. We decided not only to request new street names but also to help the council understand the gender and racial inequities we had discovered during our research. This was our third step: learning to clearly and persuasively communicate our message.

At the time of this writing, the outcome of our efforts is still pending but the kids have been promised an "exciting announcement" is soon to come. We suspect this has something to do with a new 200-acre development under construction downtown that will require new street names. We aren't sure yet if these streets will honor the work of women such as Dr. Matilda Arabella Evans, Marian Wright Edelman, and Mary McLeod Bethune, but we are hopeful, and perhaps even more importantly, I know many of the students care so much about this they will make another trip to city hall if they feel the city has not made good on its promises.

Figure 8.2
Tiffany Is Interviewed for the Local News

Not every action item we take up has a successful ending. There are times when our requests for classroom visits are ignored, our written pleas elicit vague form letters or our presentations garner us little more than a "You all did a great job!" Still, we keep at it because that's what advocacy demands. Had we not been placed on the city council agenda as invited guests, my students likely would have spoken anyway during public participation. If you're persistent enough, there's always a way. Our responsibility as classroom teachers is to make certain our students understand they *do* possess the power to change things. Yet, not everything comes easily, or immediately. We oftentimes have to commit ourselves to the long game, asking "What can we do next?"

Actions That Get at the Root Cause(s) of Social Injustice

Students don't always think to act when they see a need in their community. This isn't surprising. For most, it's unlikely they've had much experience taking action outside charitable efforts such as fundraisers or school food drives. As much as we'd like to believe experiences like a food drive help our kids grow into adults who take meaningful action, there are many reasons to suspect they won't. One is that there aren't usually opportunities for students to learn more about the issues they're addressing—such as the causes, realities, and stereotypes that surround, for instance, homelessness and hunger. Instead, schools callously turn these efforts into competitions, offering individual and class rewards for those who are the most "giving."

While remaining open to the possibility of organizing a coat drive, collecting canned goods, or donating money, we should prioritize focusing on the issue's root causes rather than immediate, short-term relief from the symptoms of injustice. For instance, organizing a school supply drive is important because it helps families under financial stress send their kids to school with the materials they need. Such efforts are both wonderful and necessary. Yet, these efforts fail to address the underlying issues at play. I find that even if children and adults can't articulate this gap, one can observe their discomfort; it's a kind of cognitive dissonance between their genuine empathy and the unspoken awareness that they aren't really changing things. After all, if they had "cured hunger" by collecting canned goods, then the canned good drive wouldn't need to happen every year. With mindful planning, a school supply drive could be accompanied by efforts to learn more about the causes of financial insecurity and then develop plans to address these—such as inviting legislators into the classroom to demand laws requiring a livable wage. When we consider action with students, we should always make sure the action is connected to the root cause(s). We don't want to put students in positions where the outcome of their actions isn't really making a difference in other people's lives but instead is just praise for their "good deeds." That creates an unhealthy savior complex, which itself perpetuates social injustice by viewing some as strong and powerful and others as weak and in need of help. We well know that those victimized by injustice do not suffer because of any personal failings but by the willfully selfish actions of some and ignorance of many others. When we don't address root causes, we allow students to think otherwise.

Inquiries That Led to Action: A Collection for Inspiration

Because we are working to create generative practices that support students to continue this work outside the classroom, our efforts to scaffold students into taking action should be responsive to their particular interests and desires. They should grow organically out of our children's discussions. This calls on us to listen closely in search of opportunities for our children to take action on their convictions. I will provide a handful of examples to illustrate what this work looks like in the classroom.

Inquiry: Representation in Children's Literature

Context: During Morning Meeting I shared a graphic illustrating the lack of representation that exists for many social groups in children's literature. After this discussion, the students and I analyzed the texts available in our own school and classroom collections and found there need to be more books that feature the diversity that shapes our world.

Turning Point: I received an email from a parent telling me her daughter, Leah, had been talking at home about a desire to address the school board to request more money for school librarians. Although she wanted school libraries to have more books in general, she was particularly interested in books that featured those who are largely missing from current collections.

Invitation: "Would you like to speak up about this? I'd be happy to help you learn more about it and prepare a speech you could read to the school board. I'll even come to the meeting with you."

Action: Because Leah's mother was a school librarian, Leah spoke with her to learn more about how funding works and the effects this has on library collections. Leah and I then brainstormed interview questions she could ask our own school librarian. We chose to focus on questions that helped her gain specific data in regard to dollar amounts and yearly books purchased (see Figure 8.3). Leah and I worked together to craft a three-minute speech that included all the information she gained from her mother and our school librarian, everything she knew about the importance of representation in children's literature, and her demands for change.

Outcome: A month later the district announced it had an unexpected surplus in the budget due to lower than expected salary and benefit

Leah

Where does the money come from to buy books?

mony comes from Scholastic Book fires every tice a Year. Some we give to PeP.

How much do you get from the district?
not sure

How much do you get from the school?
Maybe 500 $

What issues do you have as a result from not having enough money? How does it affect kids?
the issue is Ms.Watson wants to get good Books that are not in the liYbery. I think it makes the kids sad in our school because they not get the Book that they have or reading.

What would you like to see happen?
Ms.Watson would to like to make each kid have 500 $ pear stand.
↓
or a certain amount

the average book that I purchase costs 16.99 for a hard cover book.

≈ 29 books/yr.
264 kids

Figure 8.3
Leah's Interview Notes

costs and higher than expected tax revenues. They decided to award a one-time general fund budget allocation of $25 per student to each school to be used for updating library collections. Although this had been under consideration for some time, Leah's willingness to formally request such an action was well received and helped district leadership better understand the need for more consistent funding of school libraries and the inequitable nature of their collections.

• • • • •

Inquiry: Gendered Messages Embedded Within Traditional Fairy Tales

Context: Following a genre study of fairy tales, the class and I revisited these books to take a closer look at the gendered messages they contained. We analyzed each book to learn how gendered characteristics, roles, and aspirations were depicted (see Figure 8.4).

Turning Point: After finding almost all traditional fairy tales represent females as weak, vulnerable, and in need of saving, and males as strong, cunning, and capable of overcoming great obstacles, I noticed the kids began making lots of connections as they took notice of similar messages found in print ads, television shows, and movies.

	Summary	Characteristics of Female Lead	Characteristics of Male Lead	Outcome for Female Lead
Cinderella	A young girl is badly mistreated by her step-mother and step-sisters. A fairy godmother helps her attend a royal ball where she meets a prince who falls in love with her.	beautiful plain dresser honest kind poor quiet good / victim powerless	rich important powerful nice persistent royal popular	She is saved from her bad life by the prince. She marries into royalty and lives in a palace.
Rapunzel	A baby is raised by a witch who eventually locks her away in a tower. A prince finds her and falls in love with her. Eventually, he rescues her and marries her.	beautiful lonely victim powerless fearful poor	rich powerful important royal	She is saved by the prince and returns to his kingdom to be married.
Snow White	Yng girl has a mean stepmom who is jeluse of her beaui. A which Posens her whith a Plel.	Beautiful innocent chrosting	rich royal chrosting	the Princes Love saves her. they get mated & they Live in a castle.
Beauty & the Beast	A young gill has to go to the beast to liv. And she winds up liking the beast and the beast likes her.	She liked to read. She was beautiful, honest. Kind. she dint relly have a lot of money.	Angry. Upset royal rich	she saves the Prince and they get married.

Figure 8.4

Class Chart Analyzing Gendered Messages Found Within Traditional Fairy Tales

Invitation: "I bet a whole lot of people share these stories with young children without even realizing the messages they're sending. Would you like to work together to make sure others are as aware of this as we are?"

Action: We identified and wrote to people who are in a position to share traditional fairy tales with children, urging them to more carefully consider the messages these stories send young children about gendered roles and expectations. These letters were written to parents, teachers, librarians, book retailers, and book publishers. One child also wanted to alert Fox News because it was the network her mother watched each morning. None of the letters called for people to stop reading these stories. Rather, our letters asked adults to talk about these issues with children as they read fairy tales to their children so they could begin to notice these implicit messages as well.

Outcome: Letters to our immediate community (parents, teachers, and librarians) were met with a heartfelt thanks for helping them become more aware of this issue. Most said they would be more mindful of this in the future. Letters to corporations either resulted in form letters thanking the kids for their correspondence or telling them they were mistaken to think fairy tales contain such messages.

• • • • •

Inquiry: Nature of News Articles

Context: During a discussion about the overrepresentation of Black crime in the news, a student asked why the local news seems to focus so much on negative stories rather than the positive things that happen in our city. While the class continued to analyze the way Black crime is overrepresented, we launched a parallel inquiry into how news organizations select which types of stories are newsworthy.

Turning Point: The kids began paying close attention to the balance between "good" stories and "bad" stories on their own. After each negative story they would often call out, "There's another one!"

Invitation: "Are you all interested in trying to find out why news agencies do this and see if we can do something about it?"

Action: We named the potential effects of negative stories (see Figure 8.5), including the fact that overrepresentation of Black crime often feeds stereotypes, and then spent the next week studying the front page of the newspaper to see what fractional part was dedicated to these stories. Once we'd collected data, we invited a local newsperson in to present our data to them and share our concern. In doing so, we learned there is a belief that viewership is increased by stories of crime, corruption, and conflict. We were told people watch and read negative stories more often than positive stories. Afterward, we reflected on our own behaviors in the classroom and realized that, in part, this seemed to be true of us as well. Children were much more likely to spread a negative story about someone else in the classroom than a positive one. The kids admitted they often showed interest in hearing stories about someone else getting in trouble, getting hurt, or having friendship issues. We vowed to try to change this.

Outcome: For the remainder of the year we continued to talk about the types of stories we tell about others and how these affect our relationships and sense of community. Although the kids continued to miscue from time to time, such as gossiping about someone who had an emotional meltdown, we had a shared understanding to draw upon which allowed us to more effectively reflect on our choices and the effects these have not only on our classmates but our society as a whole.

Figure 8.5

Effects Negative Stories Potentially Have on Society

Watch ▶

Students Talk on Local News: Two students' current news share fuels a yearlong classroom inquiry into representation on city landmarks that eventually brings them to city hall to address the city council and local media.

To watch this video, search for "Richland Two third graders look to see more women represented on street signs" on WIS 10's local news website.

Children Find Their Voices and Solutions: Parent Cindy talks about supporting her children's activism.

Respect as Activism: Kindergarten teacher Tiffany Palmatier, on helping children identify what problems they see and what they, even as kindergartners, can do about them.

As you can see, there are times when our students' actions are intended to challenge or shape the decisions of others. At other times, our students' call to action is to more carefully consider the role *we* play in contributing to these problems. This is activism at its best—looking both inward and outward. And in creating the time and space for our students to positively transform the inequities facing their communities, we too become part of the solution. We become what our communities and profession need most in these times—agents for change.

Works Cited

Professional Works

Blow, Charles. 2018. "White Male Victimization Anxiety." *New York Times*, Oct. 10. https://www.nytimes.com/2018/10/10/opinion/trump-white-male-victimization.html.

Burke, Carolyn, Jerome Harste, and Kathy Short. 1998. *Creating Classrooms for Authors and Inquirers.* Portsmouth, NH: Heinemann.

DiAngelo, Robin. 2018. *White Fragility: Why It's So Hard for White People to Talk About Racism.* Boston: Beacon Press.

Ellis, Sarah. 2019. "Making Columbia a 'City of Women': Group Advocates for Representation on Landmarks." *The State* (SC), February 25. https://www.thestate.com/news/local/article226566014.html.

Freire, Paulo. 1970. *Pedagogy of the Oppressed.* New York: Continuum.

Gay, Geneva. 2010. *Culturally Responsive Teaching: Theory, Research, and Practice.* New York: Teachers College Press.

Hagerman, Margaret A. 2018. "Those Who Care and Those Who Don't: Children and Racism in the Trump Era." *LARB Quarterly Journal* 20. https://lareviewofbooks.org/article/care-dont-children-racism-trump-era/.

Harvey, Jonathan. 2013. "Footprints in the Field: Researcher Identity in Social Research." *Methodological Innovations* 8 (1): 86–98.

hooks, b. 1994. *Teaching to Transgress*: *Education as the Practice of Freedom.* New York: Routledge.

Howard, Tyrone C. 2010. *Why Race and Culture Matter in Schools: Closing the Achievement Gap in America's Classrooms.* New York: Teachers College Press.

Huyck, David, and Sarah Park Dahlen. 2019. "Picture This: Diversity in Children's Books 2018 Infographic." *sarahpark.com* (blog), June 19. Created in consultation with Edith Campbell, Molly Beth Griffin, K. T. Horning, Debbie Reese, Ebony Elizabeth Thomas, and Madeline Tyner, with statistics compiled by the Cooperative Children's Book Center, School of Education, University of Wisconsin-Madison: http://ccbc.education.wisc.edu/books/pcstats.asp. https://readingspark.wordpress.com/2019/06/19/picture-this-diversity-in-childrens-books-2018-infographic/.

Hyland, Ezra. 2016. "The African American Read In from NCTE." NCTE Education Talk Radio (podcast), January 17. https://www.blogtalkradio.com/edutalk/2016/01/27/the-african-american-read-in-from-ncte.

Johnston, Peter. 2004. *Choice Words: How Our Language Affects Children's Learning.* Portland, ME: Stenhouse.

Kay, Matthew R. 2018. *Not Light, but Fire: How to Lead Meaningful Race Conversations in the Classroom.* Portland, ME: Stenhouse.

Mills, Heidi. 2014. *Learning for Real: Teaching Content and Literacy Across the Curriculum.* Portsmouth, NH: Heinemann.

———. 2015. "Why Beliefs Matter." In *The Teacher You Want to Be: Essays About Children, Learning, and Teaching,* edited by Matt Glover and Ellin Oliver Keene, 33. Portsmouth, NH: Heinemann.

Mills, Heidi, Timothy O'Keefe, and Louise B. Jennings. 2004. *Looking Closely and Listening Carefully: Learning Literacy Through Inquiry.* Urbana, IL: National Council of Teachers of English.

Minor, Cornelius. 2019. *We Got This. Equity, Access, and the Quest to Be Who Our Students Need Us to Be.* Portsmouth, NH: Heinemann.

Morin, Amanda. 2019a. *Math Skills: What to Expect at Different Ages.* Understood.org. https://www.understood.org/en/learning-thinking-differences/signs-symptoms/age-by-age-learning-skills/math-skills-what-to-expect-at-different-ages.

———. 2019b. *Reading Skills: What to Expect at Different Ages.* Understood.org. https://www.understood.org/en/learning-thinking-differences/signs-symptoms/age-by-age-learning-skills/reading-skills-what-to-expect-at-different-ages.

Nieto, Sonia. 2002. *Language, Culture, and Teaching: Critical Perspectives for a New Century.* New York: Routledge.

Peirce, Charles S. 1877. "The Fixation of Belief." *Popular Science Monthly* 12: 1–15.

Teaching Tolerance. n.d. "Social Justice Standards." https://www.tolerance.org/frameworks/social-justice-standards.

Understood Team. 2019. *Writing Skills: What to Expect at Different Ages.* Understood.org. https://www.understood.org/en/learning-thinking-differences/signs-symptoms/age-by-age-learning-skills/writing-skills-what-to-expect-at-different-ages.

Children's Works

Al Abdullah, Rania, and Kelly DiPucchio. 2010. *The Sandwich Swap.* New York: Disney-Hyperion.

Alko, Selina. 2015. *The Case for Loving: The Fight for Interracial Marriage.* New York: Arthur A. Levine Books.

Beaumont, Karen. 2004. *I Like Myself!* New York: HMH Books for Young Readers.

Birtha, Becky. 2016. *Grandmama's Pride.* Park Ridge, IL: Albert Whitman & Co.

Blos, Joan W. 1990. *Old Henry.* New York: HarperCollins.

Boelts, Maribeth. 2009. *Those Shoes.* Cambridge, MA: Candlewick Press.

———. 2016. *A Bike Like Sergio's.* Somerville, MA: Candlewick Press.

Bridges, Shirin Yim. 2015. *Ruby's Wish.* San Francisco: Chronicle Books.

Bunting, Eve. 2006. *One Green Apple*. Boston: Clarion.

———. 1989. *The Wednesday Surprise*. Boston: HMH Books for Young Readers.

Byers, Grace. 2018. *I Am Enough*. New York: Balzer + Bray.

Cohn, Diana. 2002. *¡Si, Se Puede! / Yes, We Can! Janitor Strike in L.A.* El Paso, TX: Cinco Puntos Press.

Coleman, Evelyn. 1996. *White Socks Only*. Park Ridge, IL: Albert Whitman & Co.

Choi, Yangsook. 2003. *The Name Jar*. New York: Dragonflly Books.

Chung, Arree. 2018. *Mixed: A Colorful Story*. New York: Henry Holt & Co.

Danticat, Edwidge. 2015. *Mama's Nightingale: A Story of Immigration and Separation*. New York: Dial Books.

Dauvillier, Loïc. 2014. *Hidden: A Child's Story of the Holocaust*. New York: First Second.

Dempsey, Kristy. 2014. *A Dance Like Starlight*. New York: Philomel.

Dupuis, Jenny Kay, and Kathy Kacer. 2016. *I Am Not A Number*. Toronto, ON: Second Story Press.

Elliott, Zetta. 2016. *Milo's Museum*. Scotts Valley, CA: CreateSpace Independent Publishing.

Elvgren, Jennifer. 2014. *The Whispering Town*. Minneapolis: Kar-Ben Publishing.

Guerra, Jill. 2016. *Long Hair, Don't Care: A Poem About Boys with Long Hair*. www.thelovecurriculum.com.

Hamanaka, Sheila. 1999. *All the Colors of the Earth*. New York: William Morrow & Co.

Henkes, Kevin. 2008. *Chrysanthemum*. New York: Mulberry Books.

Hest, Amy. 2007. *Mr. George Baker*. Somerville, MA: Candlewick Press.

Hood, Susan. 2018. *Shaking Things Up: 14 Young Women Who Changed the World*. New York: HarperCollins.

Hubbard, Crystal. 2010. *Catching the Moon*. New York: Lee and Low Books.

Katz, Karen. 2002. *The Colors of Us*. New York: Square Fish.

Kilodavis, Cheryl. 2010. *My Princess Boy*. New York: Aladdin Books.

Lang, Suzanne. 2015. *Families, Families, Families!* New York: Random House Books for Young Readers.

Langston-George, Rebecca Ann. 2016. *For the Right to Learn: Malala Yousafzai's Story*. North Mankato, MN: Capstone.

Lears, Laurie. 1998. *Ian's Walk: A Story About Autism*. Park Ride, IL: Albert Whitman & Co.

Levinson, Cynthia. 2017. *The Youngest Marcher: The Story of Audrey Faye Hendricks, a Young Civil Rights Activist*. New York: Atheneum Books for Young Readers.

Levy, Debbie. 2016. *I Dissent: Ruth Bader Ginsburg Makes Her Mark*. New York: Simon & Schuster Books for Young Readers.

Lovell, Patty. 2001. *Stand Tall, Molly Lou Melon*. New York: G. P. Putnam's Sons.

Ludwig, Trudy. 2013. *The Invisible Boy*. New York: Knopf Books for Young Readers.

Lyon, George Ella. 2011. *Which Side Are You On? The Story of a Song*. El Paso, TX: Cinco Puntos Press.

Markel, Michelle. 2013. *Brave Girl: Clara and the Shirtwaist Makers' Strike of 1909*. New York: Balzer + Bray.

Martinez-Neal, Juana. 2018. *Alma and How She Got Her Name.* Somerville, MA: Candlewick Press.

Miller, Sharee. 2018. *Don't Touch My Hair!* New York: Little, Brown Books for Young Readers.

Miller, William. 2001. *The Bus Ride.* New York: Lee and Low Books.

Mills, Deborah, Alfredo Alva, and Claudia Navarro. 2018. *My Journey with Papa.* Cambridge, MA: Barefoot Books.

Mochizuki, Ken. 2009. *Baseball Saved Us.* New York: Lee and Low Books.

Munsch, Robert. 2005. *The Paper Bag Princess.* Toronto, ON: Annick Press.

Nyong'o, Lupita. 2019. *Sulwe.* New York: Simon and Schuster Books for Young Readers.

Palacio, R. J. 2017. *We're All Wonders.* New York: Knopf Books for Young Readers.

Pinkney, Andrea Davis. 2013. *Let It Shine: Stories of Black Women Freedom Fighters.* New York: HMH Books for Young Readers.

Polacco, Patricia. 2012. *Thank You, Mr. Falker.* New York: Philomel Books.

Ramsey, Calvin Alexander, and Gwen Strauss. 2010. *Ruth and the Green Book.* Minneapolis: Carolrhoda Books.

Stone, Tanya Lee. 2010. *Elizabeth Leads the Way: Elizabeth Cady Stanton and the Right to Vote.* New York: Square Fsh.

———. 2013. *Who Says Women Can't Be Doctors: The Story of Elizabeth Blackwell.* New York: Henry Holt.

Tarpley, Natasha Anastasia. 2001. *I Love My Hair!* New York: Little, Brown Books for Young Readers.

Thompson, Laurie Ann. 2015. *Emmanuel's Dream: The True Story of Emmanuel Ofosu Yeboah.* New York: Schwartz & Wade Books.

Tonatiuh, Duncan. 2014. *Separate Is Never Equal: Sylvia Mendez and Her Family's Fight for Desegregation.* New York: Harry N. Abrams.

Tsuchiya, Yukio. 1997. *Faithful Elephants: A True Story of Animals, People, and War.* New York: HMH Books for Young Readers.

Warren, Sarah. 2012. *Dolores Huerta: A Hero to Migrant Workers.* Tarrytown, NY: Marshall Cavendish Children.

Watson, Renee. 2012. *Harlem's Little Blackbird: The Story of Florence Mills.* New York: Random House Books for Young Readers.

Williams, Karen Lynn, and Khadra Mohammed. 2007. *Four Feet, Two Sandals.* Cambridge, UK: Eerdmans.

Williams, Mary. 2005. *Brothers in Hope: The Story of the Lost Boys of Sudan.* New York: Lee and Low Books.

Winter, Jeanette. 2017. *The World Is Not a Rectangle: A Portrait of Architect Zaha Hadid.* New York: Beach Lane Books.

———. 2019. *The Librarian of Basra.* New York: HMH Books for Young Readers.

Winter, Jonah. 2017. *Ruth Bader Ginsberg: The Case of R.B.G. vs. Inequality.* New York: Abrams Books for Young Readers.

Woodson, Jacqueline. 2012. *Each Kindness*. New York: Nancy Paulsen Books.

———. 2015. *Visiting Day*. New York: Puffin.

———. 2018. *The Day You Begin*. New York: Nancy Paulsen Books.

Yousafzai, Malala. 2017. *Malala's Magic Pencil*. New York: Little, Brown, and Company.

Zolotow, Charlotte. 1972. *William's Doll*. New York: Harper & Row.